TABLE OF CONTENTS

to accompany

Sport in Society
Issues and Controversies
Sixth Edition

Jay J. Coakley
Center for the Study of Sport and Leisure
University of Colorado

WCB McGraw-Hill

Boston, Massachusetts   Burr Ridge, Illinois   Dubuque, Iowa
Madison, Wisconsin   New York, New York   San Francisco, California   St. Louis, Missouri

WCB/McGraw-Hill

A Division of The McGraw-Hill Companies

Instructor's Manual/Test Bank to accompany
SPORT IN SOCIETY: ISSUES AND CONTROVERSIES

4 5 6 7 8 9 0 QPD/QPD 9 0 9

ISBN 0-07-092113-X

www.mhhe.com

TO THE INSTRUCTOR

This manual contains topic outlines and test questions (multiple choice and essay) for each chapter.

- **Topic outlines**

  These outlines provide quick overviews of each chapter. They highlight major topics as well as the sequence of topic coverage.

- **Multiple choice questions**

  These questions, 625 in all, are designed to test student awareness of the central points made in each chapter. An effort was made to avoid being "overly picky" when making up the questions. The focus in the questions is on concepts and ideas rather than single facts.

  I have also made a conscious effort to avoid ambiguous questions, although some of the questions are new and I have not had a chance to systematically test them for ambiguous content. To minimize misunderstandings among your students, it may be helpful for you to revise questions so they are in line with what you have emphasized in class.

- **Essay questions**

  These questions, 274 in all, are designed as *thought* questions. They require the students to pull together material from a section or series of sections in a chapter. In many cases, they also ask the student to combine material in the text with their own ideas for the purpose of dealing with everyday life issues and questions related to sport in society. These questions may be used for tests or as a basis of stimulating class discussions. I have used them on handouts given to students before they read the chapter. This helps them organize their thoughts around issues that you would like to discuss during class.

  The essay questions do not ask the students to list points or give definitions, but they do require an awareness of basic chapter content. In some cases, the essay questions deal with broad issues. Therefore, it may be necessary for you to modify them so your students will have some specific reference points as they use the material in the text to pull their thoughts together. Your modifications should also bring the questions more in line with what you have covered in class sessions.

My experience is that essay questions can be used effectively as learning devices when they are given to students in advance of the test. This enables students to focus their test preparation and to organize ideas into coherent reviews and arguments. If the class size is relatively small, you can select 5-8 questions in advance, give them to the students a week or two before the test, and then only select two to three for the students to answer during the test. This means that the students will prepare for five to eight questions, and you must read only two to three essays per student. Furthermore, you can assign different students different questions so you will not be forced to read the same essays over and over again. This makes grading less tedious and it discourages comparisons of one student to another.

Another approach is to have students write their own essay questions to supplement or replace those in this manual. This gives students an opportunity to individually structure their tests to meet their own interests. This is especially effective with groups of students who come to your class with specific interests in sports as social phenomena.

If you are teaching a course on sport and society for the first time, you may want to consider attending a conference of the North American Society for the Sociology of Sport (NASSS). Conferences are generally held during the first or second week of November in changing locations around North America. Membership forms of NASSS are regularly included in issues of the *Sociology of Sport Journal*. If it is difficult for you to obtain information through these sources, feel free to contact me by mail c/o Sociology Department, University of Colorado, Colorado Springs, CO 80933-7150. Best wishes as you use the 6th edition of *Sport in Society: Issues and Controversies* in your course.

If you have used previous editions of *Sport in Society* and find that the 6th edition no longer includes materials that you used as a basis for an important part of your course, feel free to go back to previous editions to construct handouts and make overhead transparencies that illustrate what you want to cover with your students. I do this, although I also recognize the need to continually change my course to stay current with the literature in the field. Again, let me know what materials you miss and what new materials you think should be included in the next edition.

Jay Coakley
Manitou Springs, CO

CHAPTER 1
THE SOCIOLOGY OF SPORT:
what is it and why study it?

CHAPTER OUTLINE

I. About this book

II. About this chapter

III. What is the sociology of sport?
  A. What are the differences between the sociology of sport and the psychology of sport?
  B. Using the sociology of sport
  C. Controversies created by the sociology of sport

IV. Why study sports as social phenomena?
  A. Sports are a part of people's lives
  B. Ties between sports and cultural ideology
  (BOX: "The Body and the Sociology of Sport")
  C. Sports are connected with major spheres of social life
    1. sports and family
    2. sports and the economy
    3. sports and media
    4. sports and politics
    5. sports and education
    6. sports and religion

V. What is the current status of the sociology of sport?
  A. The sociology of sport is a new field of study
  B. Organizational support for the sociology of sport
  (BOX: "Publication Sources for Sociology of Sport Research")
  C. Disagreements in the sociology of sport

VI. What are sports?
  A. An alternative approach to defining sports
  (BOX: "Sports as Contested Activities")

VII. Conclusion: why study sports?

MULTIPLE CHOICE QUESTIONS

1. The author explains that the purpose of the text is to help the reader understand the "deeper game" associated with sports. This "deeper game" refers to
   a. the hidden strategies used by coaches and athletes as they play sports
   b. the meanings underlying scores and performance statistics
   c. connections between sports and the social and cultural contexts in which they exist*
   d. the core personality characteristics of athletes and others involved in sports

2. People in the sociology of sport use their research to develop an understanding of
   a. the social worlds created around sports*
   b. the physical environments in which sports are played
   c. the differences between top athletes and others who play sports
   d. their own personal experiences in sports

3. Which of the following is least likely to be a concern of a sociologist who studies sports?
   a. the social worlds created around sports
   b. sports as social phenomena
   c. the motivation and personalities of athletes*
   d. the cultural meaning and importance of sports

4. According to the author, culture refers to ways of life that
   a. some people impose on others
   b. make some people more refined than others
   c. exist only among people from upper-class backgrounds
   d. people create through their interactions with one another*

5. The author refers to sports as cultural practices. This means that sports are
   a. human creations that come into being as people interact with each other*
   b. much the same in all cultures
   c. unchanging through history
   d. activities which must be done over and over before people can really enjoy them

6. Which of the following is least likely to be studied by someone in the sociology of sport?
   a. the physical demands of different sports*
   b. the relationship between sports and religion
   c. the ways that sports are included into social life
   d. the organization and meanings of sports

7. The sociology of sport differs from the psychology of sport in that sociologists are more likely than psychologists to focus on
   a. the personal troubles of individual athletes in elite sports
   b. issues such as self-esteem and confidence
   c. the performance records of athletes with different personalities
   d. how sport programs are organized and how athletes fit into that organization*

8. As opposed to a psychologist, a sociologist would study burnout among athletes in terms of the
   a. power athletes have to make decisions about their lives*
   b. stress that exists in athletes' lives
   c. stress management strategies used by athletes
   d. personal troubles of individual athletes

9. When sociologists study problems in sports, their recommendations are sometimes controversial because they often call for changes in
   a. the people who participate in sports
   b. the structure and organization of sports*
   c. how sports are funded and supported
   d. strategies that athletes use to promote their own interests

10. If someone in the sociology of sport studied sport participation among women in countries around the world, attention would most likely be devoted to the following?
    a. the physical skills of women compared to men
    b. the need for women to take sports more seriously
    c. women's access to the time and resources needed to play sports*
    d. the ability of women to grasp the complex rules in many sports

11. After reading the chapter, which of the following do you think someone in the sociology of sport would be most likely to study in a research project on violence in sports?
    a. the personality characteristics of those involved in the violence
    b. the motivations of the individuals who played leadership roles in the violence
    c. the connections between violence and the organization of social life and social relationships*
    d. the amount of stress experienced by those who eventually participated in the violence

12. The author explains that sports should be studied as social phenomena because sports are
    a. closely tied to cultural ideology in society*
    b. less important today than in the past
    c. one of the few activities unrelated to social class
    d. generally ignored by the media

13. The gender logic that was commonly accepted in sports in the past tended to emphasize that
    a. being female meant being a failure in sports*
    b. women were naturally more aggressive than men
    c. girls and boys should learn to play sports together
    d. competent women athletes were sexually attractive

14. Which of the following is a false statement about cultural ideology?
    a. Cultural ideology consists of ideas that people use to make sense out of the world
    b. Cultural ideology is stable and unchanging in most societies around the world*
    c. Cultural ideology refers to the underlying logic of how people live their lives
    d. Cultural ideology emerges as people struggle over the meanings and importance of things and events in their lives

15. When the author says that the human body is social, this means that
    a. muscular bodies have always been defined in positive ways
    b. all bodies are basically the same from one culture to another
    c. bodies have an essential physicality that never changes
    d. the meanings associated with bodies and body parts are grounded in culture*

16. In the discussion of the connection between sports and the major spheres of life in industrial societies, the author points out that
    a. sports usually affect family life in negative ways
    b. the media have enabled some athletes to become global entertainers*
    c. large corporations today are less likely to sponsors sports than they were in the past
    d. sports are related to the economy and education but not to politics or religion

17. According to the text, studying the sociology of sport is important because
    a. people in industrial countries spend more money on sports than on food or housing
    b. sport events and sport organizations offer useful settings for learning about behavior and culture*
    c. using sociological research has helped coaches improve win-loss records in team sports
    d. athletes participate in society in different ways than those who are not athletes

18. The lack of scholarly attention given to sports in the past was at least partially related to the fact that
   a. people who teach physical education and sociology have seldom participated in sports themselves
   b. studying sport was not something that contributed to the careers of those in physical education and sociology*
   c. sport participation in the past often occurred in private settings where behavior could not be studied
   d. Euro-American cultures never made clear distinctions between physical and intellectual activities

19. According to the author's explanation, people who refer to themselves as "sport sociologists" are usually those who
   a. have more of an interest in understanding behavior than in understanding the organization of sports
   b. are more concerned with contributing knowledge to the sport sciences than to sociology*
   c. prefer using a critical transformation model over a scientific expert model of doing science
   d. do research on problems in the lives of those who lack power and resources

20. Not everyone in the sociology of sport sees the field in the same way. Some sociologists favor a "critical transformation" model while others favor a "scientific expert" model of doing science. According to the author, one of the dangers of using the "scientific expert" model is that it sometimes leads to an overemphasis on
   a. teaching graduate students rather than doing research
   b. doing research dealing with social problems
   c. doing research that fosters the interests of people with power and money*
   d. the issues of human freedom and revolutionary social change

21. In the definition of sports provided in the chapter, which of the following factors was *not* considered crucial in identifying an activity as a sport?
   a. the type of activity involved
   b. the subjective orientations of the participants
   c. the amount of risk involved*
   d. the conditions under which the activity takes place

22. According to the definition of sports provided in the chapter, which of the following would be an example of a sport?
   a. two friends jogging together every morning
   b. racing in the Indianapolis 500*
   c. playing dodge ball during school recess
   d. playing chess in a city tournament

23. To be classified as a sport according to the definition in the chapter, an activity must involve
    a. complex cognitive skills combined with complex physical skills
    b. institutionalized competition and physical skills*
    c. an emphasis on cooperation and teamwork
    d. psychological challenges and cognitive strategies

24. When applied to physical activities, the term institutionalization implies the existence of
    a. a formalized and patterned structure*
    b. at least two teams of individuals
    c. irrational behavior on the part of participants
    d. games controlled by players and coaches

25. Using the definition of sport provided in the chapter, it could be said that a game becomes a sport when
    a. the learning of skills is informal and unorganized
    b. rules are no longer defined in strict terms
    c. rule enforcement becomes a low-priority issue
    d. the organizational aspects of the game become important*

26. According to the author's explanation of the definition of sport provided in the chapter, one of the ways to distinguish sports from play is to identify the participants' motives for involvement. In the chapter, it is pointed out that involvement in
    a. play is motivated by both intrinsic and extrinsic rewards
    b. sport participation is motivated by both intrinsic and extrinsic rewards*
    c. both play and sport is motivated by extrinsic rewards
    d. both play and sport is motivated by both intrinsic and extrinsic rewards

27. According to the author's explanation of the definition of sport provided in the chapter, a sport is in danger of becoming a spectacle when
    a. the element of play is overemphasized
    b. spectators are eliminated from the event
    c. athletes play for themselves rather than the spectators
    d. pleasing the audience becomes all-important*

28. According to the author, the definition of sports given in the chapter is
    a. the definition used by all people in all societies
    b. designed to encompass all physical activities
    c. helpful in distinguishing sports from related activities*
    d. the only correct way to define sport if you want to study it

29.	According to the author, one of the problems with the definition of sport provided in the chapter is that it might lead some sociologists to
	a.	ignore the physical activities of people who lack the resources to formally organize their games*
	b.	ask too many critical questions about sports and destroy the enjoyment of both athletes and spectators
	c.	focus too much attention on the games of people in low income groups
	d.	ignore the political importance of sports in society

30.	Some sociologists do not use a strict definition of sports to guide their research. Instead, they use an alternative approach in which they ask the question:
	a.	when do sports become socially significant?
	b.	why do all cultures have competitive sports?
	c.	what gets to count as sport in society?*
	d.	why do children prefer play over sports?

31.	When sociologists say that sports are "contested activities," they mean that
	a.	all sports involved some form of contest or competition
	b.	sports exist to enable people to have contests with each other
	c.	people in any society must compete with each other to play sports
	d.	people struggle over what sports could and should be in society*

ESSAY QUESTIONS

1.	In a conversation with your parents, you mention that you're taking a sociology of sport class at college. Your father accuses you of wasting his money and your time on a frivolous course. It is up to you to explain to him that his money and your time is not being wasted. What would you say in your explanation?

2.	After you take this course in the sociology of sport, you decide to take a course on the psychology of sport. What would you expect to be the differences between the two courses? Give examples of how sociologists and psychologists would study sport topics, and indicate what concepts they might use in their research.

3.	Imagine you are a sociologist or physical educator and you want to offer a sociology of sport course in your department. How would you present your case to your colleagues in the department? It is up to you to convince them that the course would be a worthwhile addition to the departmental curriculum.

4.	Some sociologists study sports because sports are tied closely to cultural ideology in society. Explain what is meant by "ideology" and then show how sports are related to ideas about gender, including dominant ideas about masculinity and femininity.

5.   Much recent research in the sociology of sport focuses on the body in social and cultural terms rather than biological terms. This research is based on the notion that the body is socially constructed and given meaning within the context of culture. Explain what this means and list some of the issues that sociologists might study as they focus on the body as a social phenomenon.

6.   One of your friends is surprised when you tell her that the sociology of sport has only been in existence for the last 30 years or so. She asks you why it wasn't developed earlier. How would you respond to her question?

7.   You must choose one of two teachers for your sociology of sport course. One favors a "critical transformation" model in the readings and course discussions, while the other favors a "scientific expert" model. Which teacher would you choose? Explain the issues you considered in making your choice.

8.   Some sociologists think that a precise definition of sports is needed so they can distinguish sports from other phenomena that have different social dynamics and social implications. Using the definition of sport given in the chapter, identify which of the following activities would be classified as sports. Give reasons for your classifications.
- racing in the Indianapolis 500   - the Super Bowl
- skiing with friends at a resort   - jogging every morning
- a handball tournament at the YMCA   - chess in a school tournament
- bowling in a Friday night league   - taking an aerobics class

9.   When a physical activity becomes a sport, it changes in a number of ways. Using any activity with which you are familiar, explain what happens as the activity becomes a sport.

10.   Some people say that playing with a Frisbee is a sport, others say it is simply an enjoyable physical activity. Under what conditions would playing with a Frisbee be a sport according to the definition provided in the text? Give some examples of when it would be a sport and when it would not be a sport.

11.   According to the definitions provided in the text, wrestling is sometimes a form of play, sometimes a sport, and sometimes a spectacle. Give examples of wrestling in each of these three forms and discuss the factors that lead it to be classified in each of these three categories.

12.   Which of the major sports in the U.S. is closest to becoming a spectacle? Give reasons for your choice and illustrate what would be necessary to prevent that sport from becoming a spectacle.

13.   In a survey of the attitudes of adults in the U.S., it was found that over half the population thinks that television sports have become too much like spectacles. What does this mean and how would you explain why people think this way?

14. Instead of trying to define "sports," some scholars focus their attention on studying what gets to count as a sport in society and whose sports count the most. What is the advantage of taking this approach to defining sports when studying sports in society?

15. Street roller hockey is growing in popularity among middle-class boys and girls in many suburban communities around the country. Jump rope is growing in popularity among low-income, African American girls in many large cities. Which of these two activities is most likely to become a sport according to the criteria and definition outlined in the chapter? Give at least two reasons for your choice.

16. The author makes the case that sports are contested activities. This means that people have differing ideas about what sports could and should be in society, and they struggle over whose ideas will prevail. Explain some of the issues over which people have struggled in recent years as they determine what sports are and how they will be included in their lives.

CHAPTER 2
USING SOCIAL THEORIES:
what can they tell us about sports in society?

CHAPTER OUTLINE

I.   Theories in sociology

II.   Theories about sports and society
    A.   Functionalist theory: sports are an inspiration
        1.   Functionalist theory and research on sports
        2.   Limitations of functionalist theory
    B.   Conflict theory: sports are an opiate
        1.   Conflict theory and research on sports
        2.   Limitations of conflict theory
    C.   Critical theories: sports are social constructions
    (BOX: "Feminist theories: a critical look at gender and sports")
        1.   Critical theory and research on sports
            a.   Example #1: creating alternatives to dominant forms of sports
            b.   Example #2: the social construction of masculinity in sports
            c.   Example #3: sport rituals and social life in a small town
    (BOX: "Sports are more than reflections of society")
        2.   Limitations of critical theory
    D.   Interactionist theories: sports are meaningful interaction
        1.   Interactionist theories and research on sports
            a.   Example #1: the complex process of becoming an athlete
            b.   Example #2: the meaning of Little League baseball
            c.   Example #3: the meaning of pain in an athlete's life
        2.   Limitations of interactionist theories

III. Using sociological theories: a comparison
    A.   Applications of functionalist theory
    B.   Applications of conflict theory
    C.   Applications of critical theories
    D.   Applications of interactionist theories

IV.   Summary and conclusions: is there a best theoretical approach to use when studying sports?

MULTIPLE CHOICE QUESTIONS

1. The origins of modernist science can be traced back to the "Enlightenment Period" in European history. Modernism in the social sciences is based on the idea that
    a. a combination of religious faith and hard work would lead to a perfect world
    b. humans could create a just and efficient world through rationality and science*
    c. evolution would lead to forms of social progress that would benefit the world as a whole
    d. scientific truth was a myth that interfered with real social progress

2. Although many sociologists in the past have sought a general theory of social life, a growing number of sociologists today have not joined the search for general theories because
    a. the search often leads sociologists to ignore the diversity and contradictions that are a part of everyday life*
    b. there are no financial payoffs connected with such a search
    c. they are not interested in discovering knowledge that might be used to influence human life
    d. the research involved in the search is too difficult and time-consuming

3. The diversity of theoretical approaches used in sociology is due to a series of important changes in today's world. Which of the following is *not* one of the changes discussed by the author?
    a. women have raised questions about theories that have ignored them and their experiences
    b. increased awareness of people and events around the globe has forced people to recognize the importance of non-Eurocentric viewpoints
    c. the growth and development of communications technology has changed ideas about "reality"
    d. people with power and privilege have abandoned the use of science in their lives*

4. Many sociologists have used functionalist theory to understand society and social life. When a functionalist theory is used, sociologists look for the ways that sport contributes to
    a. the smooth operation of society as a whole*
    b. the development of strong leaders within society
    c. a general societal commitment to democratic principles
    d. the existence of conflict and change with societies

5. Those who use functionalist theory assume that certain things must happen for any social system to operate smoothly. Which of the following is not one of things that must happen?
   a. there must be opportunities for people in the system to release tension and frustration in harmless ways
   b. there must be mechanisms for responding to changes occurring outside the system without disrupting order inside the system
   c. there must be mechanisms for bringing people together and establishing integrated social relationships
   d. there must be organizational structures that enable a few people to control the lives of the masses*

6. Which of the following statements about sport would *not* be made by a functionalist?
   a. the popularity of sport in society is proof that it contributes to the smooth operation of that society
   b. participation in sport teaches people about important values in their society
   c. sport provides a setting for changes which can effect some groups more than others*
   d. sport helps people in society to release tension and frustration harmlessly

7. When sociologists use functionalist theory to guide their research on sports, one of the issues that they have focused on is
   a. the relationship between sport and the distribution of power in society
   b. social interaction and the meanings associated with sport and sport participation
   c. the connection between sports and social conflict in society
   d. the relationship between sports and social order in society*

8. When the limitations of functionalist theory were discussed in the chapter, the author pointed out that those who use functionalist theory tend to
   a. overemphasize the negative aspects of sport
   b. mistakenly assume that society is held together by coercion and exploitation
   c. mistakenly assume that sport equally serves the needs of all groups in the social system*
   d. ignore the extent to which people in any society hold common values

9. When sociologists use conflict theory to study society and social life, they are primarily concerned with
   a. class relations and the social processes revolving around economic power in society*
   b. the extent to which shared values exist among people in the society
   c. how the parts of society fit together in supportive ways
   d. how shared values and conflicts of interest can exist simultaneously in a society

10.	According to conflict theory, the existence and popularity of sport in capitalist societies is related to the
	a.	physical abilities of workers
	b.	efficiency of production processes
	c.	need for workers to escape alienating jobs*
	d.	control that workers have over their jobs in industry

11.	When sociologists have used conflict theory to guide their research on sport, one topic they have focused on is how
	a.	athletes are motivated by things other than money
	b.	sports can be used by economic elites to control the masses of workers in society*
	c.	sports are used to eliminate economic differences among people in society
	d.	the meanings associated with sports vary from one group to another

12.	Unlike functionalist theory, conflict theory is likely to lead people to emphasize that
	a.	economic factors are the driving force in society*
	b.	sports are an inspiration in society
	c.	system needs must be met for society to operate smoothly
	d.	social inequality is needed to motivate people in society

13.	Which of the following statements is *not* likely to be made by someone using conflict theory? "Within a capitalist system, sport
	a.	distorts people's perception of reality"
	b.	creates radical political awareness in society"*
	c.	intensifies commercialism and materialism in society"
	d.	perpetuates economic inequalities in society"

14.	According to the author, many beginning students in the sociology of sport are not comfortable using conflict theory because they think it is
	a.	very complex and difficult to understand
	b.	negative and critical of sports and society*
	c.	right-wing in terms of its political implications
	d.	not relevant in societies where money is as important as it is in most industrial societies today

15.	When the limitations of conflict theory were discussed, the author pointed out that a major weakness of conflict theory is that it
	a.	focuses too much on issues related to gender and race
	b.	underemphasizes the impact of economic factors on the structure of sport
	c.	ignores cases where sport participation involves empowering experiences for individuals and groups*
	d.	ignores professional and other elite forms of sports

16. Few sociologists today use functionalist theory or conflict theory to guide their study of sports. A growing number of sociologists use various forms of critical theory. Critical theories primarily emphasize
    a. the inspirational character of sport participation
    b. the connection between sports and power struggles over how social life is and should be organized*
    c. the relationship between sports and "market needs" in capitalist societies
    d. how sports are simply a reflection of society

17. When critical theories are used to analyze the relationship between sports and society, sports are seen as
    a. a reflection of the needs of the economic system in society
    b. a reflection of the general system needs in society
    c. an outgrowth of the power relations of people in society*
    d. a set of activities unrelated to other spheres of social life

18. When looking at the relationship between sport and society, a critical theorist would be concerned with how
    a. the true nature of sport has been distorted in modern societies
    b. the organization of sports are dictated by the needs of society
    c. athletes are victimized through their sport experiences
    d. sports can be sites for promoting changes in the organization of social life*

19. The author notes that critical theories can sometimes be confusing because they are based on three complex ideas. Which of the following is *not* one of those ideas?
    a. that agreement and conflict can exist simultaneously in social life
    b. that shared values are never permanent in any society
    c. that the causes of conflict in society change over time and from place to place
    d. that all social systems have built-in mechanisms for maintaining balance and agreement among people*

20. Feminist theories are important forms of critical theories. Feminist theories have generally grown out of a dissatisfaction with intellectual traditions that fail to recognize the extent to which
    a. family life and religion is important in any society
    b. women have power and control in all aspects of social life
    c. men's values and experiences had shaped science and the production of scientific knowledge*
    d. women have natural abilities for understanding social life and social relationships

16

21. According to the author, a primary difference between liberal feminists and radical feminists is that liberal feminists often limit most of their attention to
    a. issues of discrimination and unequal opportunities*
    b. the need for changing the structure of social life
    c. the advantages of "feminizing" all of social life
    d. issues that will gain them power and status in society

22. According to the author, radical feminists studying sports would question the merits of
    a. equality and democracy in sport organizations
    b. women's participation in sports that give priority to and reproduce traditional male values*
    c. sports emphasizing the values and experiences of women in society
    d. sports promoting cooperation and self-fulfillment

23. When feminists describe sports as "gendered" activities, they mean that the standards used to evaluate success and qualifications in sports are
    a. created by men and women working together in sport organizations
    b. applied by women to men and by men to women
    c. used to promote new ways of thinking about what is masculine and what is feminine
    d. socially constructed around a limited set of male values and experiences*

24. According to the author, many of the sport-related questions asked by feminists are questions that
    a. men have been asking for many years both in an out of sports
    b. challenge the very foundation of many sports and sport organizations*
    c. are unrelated to important issues in sports today
    d. ignore men and men's involvement in sports and sport organizations

25. According to the author, the commonly made statement that "sports are reflections of society" is
    a. not supported in any of the research done in the sociology of sport
    b. applies to race and gender issues, but not to other issues discussed in the sociology of sport
    c. is not very helpful for those wanting to take an in-depth, critical look at sports in society*
    d. likely to inspire people to want to change sports

26. According to the author, the ultimate goal of research done by people using critical theories is
    a. understanding the needs of social systems
    b. describing the essential goodness of human beings
    c. making social life more efficient
    c. producing changes in social life*

27. The summary of Birrell and Richter's study of a women's softball league (included in the section on critical theory) was used by the author to emphasize that
    a. sports are created by people, and therefore can be changed by people*
    b. sports have an unchanging essence that people can only discover through sport participation
    c. when women participate in sports, they play in the same ways men play
    d. men and women can play certain sports together if women stand up for their rights

28. The data collected by Michael Messner in his study of male athletes indicated that when men play sports at elite levels of competition, they become involved in processes through which they
    a. establish intimate relationships with each other
    b. question the whole idea of male superiority
    c. become motivated to change sports and make them less competitive and aggressive
    d. enhance their public status and create nonintimate bonds with other men*

29. After doing a careful study of sport rituals and social life in a small town in Texas, Doug Foley concluded that
    a. high school sports brought everyone in the community together into a cohesive group
    b. it was difficult to use sports to challenge the way social life was organized*
    c. sports, especially high school football, promoted democracy and equality in the town
    d. sports were used by women and minorities to gain power and control in the community as a whole

30. According to the author, one of the major criticisms of critical theory is that it
    a. is too similar to functionalism in its emphasis on "system needs"
    b. generates so much pessimism that most people do not want to use it
    c. does not provide a single, understandable framework for analyzing the sport-society relationship*
    d. focuses too much on the everyday lives of people in society

31. Interactionist theories have recently become more widely used to guide research in the sociology of sport. These theories emphasize that social life and the behavior of human beings is based on
    a. social inequality and power relations in society
    b. general social forces in the economic and political spheres of life
    c. how people give meaning to their lives and make decisions based on those meanings*
    d. personality and the distribution of different personality types in a society

32. The study done by Donnelly and Young (and summarized in the chapter) emphasized that becoming a serious athlete depends on
   a. having the motivation to play sports when things get tough and there is nobody there to provide support
   b. consistent social support leading to self-identification as an athlete and acceptance into a group of athletes*
   c. support coming from a particular family member with the resources to control the person's training
   d. being able to ignore the influence of peer groups and avoid connections with other athletes

33. Gary Alan Fine's study of boys in youth baseball leagues (summarized in the chapter) led him to discover that the boys in these leagues were most often concerned with
   a. being socially accepted by their male peers*
   b. being respected by adults in the community
   c. understanding the moral lessons presented to them by parents and coaches
   d. establishing close relationships with girls and younger boys

34. Tim Curry's study of the meaning of pain in an athlete's life (summarized in the chapter) emphasized that over time, an athlete comes to see pain and injury as
   a. something to be avoided at all costs
   b. caused by carelessness and lack of training
   c. a routine part of sport participation*
   d. self-destructive aspects of the sport experience

35. According to the author, one of the main weaknesses of interactionist theories is that they do not explain how
   a. structured forms of inequality operate in sports and social life as a whole*
   b. different people define sports in different ways
   c. sport participation is tied to issues of social interaction and identity
   d. individuals come to be involved in sports and why they stay involved

36. According to the author, sociological theories are especially useful for those who are
   a. interested in bringing about social change*
   b. concerned with keeping things in society much the way they are now
   c. more concerned with trivial details about everyday life than with general questions about the social world
   d. unconcerned with practical knowledge about everyday life

37. The author makes the case that the major difference between sociological theories and our personal theories about social life is that
    a.   personal theories are tools and sociological theories are ends in themselves
    b.   personal theories can help us make choices while sociological theories cannot
    c.   sociological theories are publicly subjected to systematic testing and criticism while personal theories are not*
    d.   sociological theories are not useful for individuals while personal theories are

38. If sociologists used a functionalist approach as a guide for making policy recommendations related to sports, their recommendations would probably call for
    a.   the development of players' unions
    b.   more organized programs and more supervision for athletes*
    c.   increased choices for the participants in sports
    d.   less structured and less organized sport experiences

39. The sport-related policy recommendations of those using conflict theory as their guide are likely to emphasize
    a.   the ways in which sports could become more organized
    b.   the need to eliminate the profit motive in sport*
    c.   the need for more spectator sports in capitalist societies
    d.   the reasons why players' unions should be abolished

40. The sport-related policy recommendations of those using critical theories as their guide are likely to call for changes leading to
    a.   increased choices and opportunities for all sport participants*
    b.   revisions in who controls sports
    c.   fewer organized sports for everyone
    d.   the use of scientific guidelines to organize sport more efficiently

41. The sport-related policy recommendations of those using interactionist theories as their guide are likely to call for changes leading to
    a.   clearer definitions of the meanings of sports and sport experiences
    b.   opportunities for athletes to raise questions about the organization and meaning of sport participation*
    c.   questions about the economic organization of society as a whole
    d.   new ideas on how to shape the personalities of athletes

42. According to the author, if your goal is to simply understand as much as possible about sports as social phenomena, it would be best to
    a.   use two or more theoretical approaches*
    b.   abandon conflict theory and functionalism
    c.   use functionalism more than either of the other two theories
    d.   use critical theory to analyze capitalist societies and conflict theory to analyze socialist societies

ESSAY QUESTIONS

1. Sociologists use a number of different theoretical approaches as they study sport in society. Explain why theories are important and why multiple theoretical approaches are used by sociologists.

2. Imagine yourself as the director of the Parks and Recreation Department in a large city. The city council has just threatened to withdraw funds for all your organized sport programs. In arguing for continuation of the funds, which theoretical approach would be most helpful for you? What would your argument be when you came in front of the council to make your case for the continuation of funds?

3. You are a city councilperson representing a low-income minority district in the city. The rest of the members of council want to use city tax money to build a new tennis stadium to host major tennis tournaments during the year. In arguing against this expenditure, which theoretical framework would be most useful to you? What would your argument be when you made your statement to the rest of council?

4. It has just been announced that a new three-rink ice arena will be built in your town. It will be funded through a combination of public, private, and foundation money. You have been hired by a civic group to do a study of how the decision was made to devote resources to this project rather than other projects that might benefit the community. Which theoretical framework would you use to guide your study? Give reasons for choosing this framework.

5. Your sociology of sport instructor has invited to your class a sociologist who uses functionalist theory to explain and study sports. This person will present a lecture on how sports are sources of inspiration in societies around the world. You want to ask some challenging questions to the speaker after his presentation. What three questions would you ask and why would you ask them?

6. Your sociology of sport instructor has invited to your class a conflict theorist. She will give a lecture on how sports are the opiate of the masses in industrial society. You want to ask some challenging questions to the speaker after her presentation. What three questions would you ask and why would you ask them?

7. Critical theories comes in many different forms. But if a group of critical theorists came together in a seminar, they would agree on a number of issues related to how they approach the study of society. Imagine such a seminar (including Susan Birrell or Diana Richter, Michael Messner, and Doug Foley) and explain where there would be agreement among the participants.

8. Your sociology of sport instructor has invited to your class a feminist theorist. He will give a lecture on gender issues and sports. You hear that this person is more of a radical feminist than a liberal feminist. What are the issues that you could expect this person to emphasize in his presentation? Some people in your class feel threatened by what they think this person might say. Are their feelings justified? Explain why or why not.

9. A friend of yours is taking a sociology of sport course at another university. When you get together during the summer after you have both completed the courses, you ask her what she learned in her course. She says that the most important thing she learned was that sport is a reflection of society. You tell her that in your class the instructor said that the idea that sport was simply a reflection of society was an oversimplified way of looking at the sport-society relationship. She asks you why and you have to come up with a good explanation. What would you say?

10. You have just been appointed to a committee which has been asked to develop a set of policy recommendations for changing the organized youth sport programs in your town. There are three other people on the committee. One views sports in terms of functionalist theory, one in terms of conflict theory, and one in terms of feminist theory. Explain the recommendations you would expect from each of them and then say who you would agree with when it came to writing your final report for the committee.

11. Your sociology of sport instructor has invited to your class a person who uses interactionist theory to study sports and sport participation. He will give a lecture on the process of becoming an athlete and will refer to the studies used as examples in the chapter (by Donnelly and Young, by Fine, and by Curry). What are the issues that you could expect this person to emphasize in his presentation and what kinds of questions would you want to ask this person during the question/answer period?

12. You are a parent with two children. One is a 10th-grader and one is an 8th-grader. On a Sunday afternoon, they complain that they have nothing to do. You tell them that they should go to the school gym and play basketball or volleyball. They tell you the school gym is closed every weekend. You can't believe that someone could make such a stupid decision. Using critical theory, develop a set of questions you would ask about this issue of closed gymnasiums. What would be your predictions on why the gyms are closed? Who do you think would benefit the most from such a decision?

13. The people at your university have probably used a functionalist approach when they have made decisions about the intercollegiate programs sponsored by the school. Use any of the theoretical approaches discussed in the chapter as a basis for identifying and discussing the problems associated with your school's intercollegiate program, and for making suggestions on how the program could be changed.

14.   One of the assignments in your sociology of sport course is to write a paper in which you use a particular theoretical approach to understand a particular aspect of sport as a social phenomenon. What would you choose to study and which theory or theories would be most helpful to you as you did your study?

CHAPTER 3
A LOOK AT THE PAST:
how have sports changed throughout history?

CHAPTER OUTLINE

I.   An opening note on history

II.   Sports vary by time and place

III.   Games in ancient Greece: beyond the myths (1000 BC - 100 BC)

IV.   Roman sport events: spectacles and gladiators (100 BC - 500 AD)

V.   Tournaments and games during the Middle Ages: separation of the masters and masses (500 AD - 1300)

VI.   The Renaissance, Reformation, and Enlightenment: games as diversions (1300 - 1800)
        (BOX: "Lessons from history: distorted views of sports among Native Americans")
        A.   The Renaissance
        B.   The Reformation
        C.   The Enlightenment

VII.   The Industrial Revolution: the emergence of standardized sport forms (1780 - present)
        A.   The early years: limited time and space
        B.   The later years: changing interests, values, and opportunities
                1.   The seeds of new meanings
                2.   The growth of elite, competitive sports in the United States: 1880 - 1920
                        a.   Power and wealth in action
                        b.   Ideas about sport participation and "character development"
                        c.   Organized sports and ideas about masculinity and femininity
                        d.   Organized sports and ideas about skin color and ethnicity
                        e.   Organized sports and ideas about age and disability
                        f.   1880 to 1920 - a key period
                3.   Since the 1920s: the struggles continue
        (BOX: "The characteristics of high-profile, organized, competitive sports")

VIII. Conclusion: looking at sports at different times and different places

_____

MULTIPLE CHOICE QUESTIONS

1. Instead of trying to provide an overview of all sports history around the entire world, the author writes the chapter as
    a. an explanation of why sports have not changed much over time from one culture to the next
    b. a story about progress and the gradual improvement of sports over time
    c. a series of stories about struggles over the organization and meaning of sports*
    d. a chronological account of how traditional sports have been maintained through the years

2. According to the author, the fact that more people around the globe are now playing similar types of physical games is an indication that
    a. global power relations have an impact on the sponsorship and promotion of certain sport forms*
    b. sports are naturally evolving along the same path of development around the world
    c. modernization and cultural progress are very powerful processes that occur in all cultures
    d. human beings all have similar needs that are expressed through particular types of competitive games

3. The historical overview provided in the chapter is based on the assumption that throughout human history, sports have been integrally related to
    a. the political and social structures dominant at any point in time*
    b. geographical factors affecting outdoor activities
    c. physiological capabilities within various populations
    d. the nature of religious organization within societies

4. The author notes that during prehistoric times, the physical activities engaged in by people were usually
    a. forms of political confrontation
    b. forms of religious worship tied to sacred rituals and ceremonies*
    c. rites of passage for both young males and females
    d. forms of economic activity serving material purposes in society

5. According to the author, the people who have had the greatest impact on sports throughout history have usually been those who
    a. are the best athletes
    b. manufacture the equipment for sports
    c. have the most power in the society*
    d. come from families with traditions of sport participation

6. Which of the following would *not* be an accurate description of the games played by the early Greeks?
   a. the participation of women was given a very low priority
   b. the games were tied to the achievements of Greek gods
   c. most of the participants came from or were sponsored by wealthy Greek families
   d. warrior sports were banned from the games because they were dangerous for participants*

7. The author explains that Greek games took on political significance, the athletes who participated in them
   a. began to form organizations to help them bargain for their rights*
   b. came exclusively from upper-income families in Greek society
   c. developed generalized skills across a wide range of activities
   d. usually became philosophers and intellectuals within Greek society

8. According to the information presented in the boxed section, Greek sports differed from the high-profile, organized, competitive sports of today in that they
   a. had highly developed administrative structures
   b. did not involve measurements and record-keeping*
   c. seldom involved direct competition between athletes
   d. were able to avoid professionalization and maintain pure amateur sports

9. According to the author's discussion of Roman sport events, Roman leaders generally used those events
   a. as diversions for the masses*
   b. to emphasize the qualities of individualism and specialized skills
   c. to encourage the participation of citizens in governmental affairs
   d. to give lower-income people a chance to work, buy property, and pass property rights on to their children

10. The Romans who criticized the sport spectacles in their own communities based their criticisms primarily on the idea that no good could come out of events during which
    a. slaves were exploited
    b. Christians were put to death for the pleasure of others
    c. people from different social classes mixed with one another and watched "common people" perform*
    d. high-ranking officials lowered themselves to the status of average citizens

11. According to the information presented in the boxed section, Roman sport events differed from the high-profile, organized, competitive sports of today in that they seldom involved
    a. the recording of outstanding accomplishments*
    b. rationalization and bureaucratization
    c. clearly defined distinctions made between men and women athletes
    d. physical skills requiring speed or strength

12. The author explains that during the Middle Ages, the games played by European peasants were primarily influenced by a combination of
    a. local customs and the Catholic Church*
    b. Greek philosophy and romantic ideals
    c. political relationships and cultural traditions
    d. community rivalries and the need for exercise

13. When the games of Europe's upper classes are compared with the games of the peasants during the Middle Ages, it is seen that they are
    a. based on the same general game models
    b. distinctively different from one another*
    c. grounded in different sets of religious beliefs
    d. both very similar to modern sports in a number of ways

14. The author notes that through a good part of the medieval period, the most popular sporting events in Europe consisted of a series of war games. These events were designed to
    a. recruit peasants into the military
    b. train women to protect their homes and children
    c. maintain military readiness among upper-class males*
    d. enable knights and nobles to frighten peasants and maidens with their awesome abilities

15. European women during the medieval period were not as involved in physically active games as were men. According to the author, their opportunities were restricted by a combination of
    a. physical weakness and the need to serve political roles in the community
    b. homophobic attitudes and beliefs that women were not competitive
    c. child-centered home lives and a lack of free time
    d. male-centered family structures and the teachings of the Roman Catholic Church*

16. According to the information presented in the boxed section, sports in Medieval Europe differed from the high-profile, organized, competitive sports of today in many ways. Which of the following is *not* one of the differences? Unlike so-called Modern sports,
    a. Medieval sports lacked specialization and organization
    b. Medieval sports never involved measuring and recording athletic achievements*
    c. Medieval sports were not open to all competitors, regardless of social status
    d. Medieval sports were secular events and had no real religious significance

17. The growth of Calvinism and Puritanism during the Protestant Reformation in Europe and North America (early 1500s to the late 1600s) was generally associated with
    a. a growth in the popularity of sports and games, especially on the Sabbath
    b. increased sport participation among women but not among men
    c. negative attitudes about sports and games, especially when they were played on the Sabbath*
    d. the conversion of games and sports into work activities by the members of the upper classes

18. Sport activities in Europe and North America in particular became increasingly organized during the Enlightenment period (1700 - 1800). But unlike the high-profile, organized, competitive sports of today they were
    a. based on the idea that competition was bad
    b. organized by religious groups
    c. often inhumane and dangerous
    d. defined strictly as diversions*

19. According to the analysis by Joseph Oxendine (in the boxed section in the chapter), reporting on the lives and sport activities of Native Americans over the past 200 years has been seriously distorted because
    a. white Europeans were more interested in helping Native Americans improve their quality of life than in studying their lifestyles
    b. white Europeans were seldom allowed to observe Native American games in their traditional religious forms*
    c. most Native American groups did not play physical games regularly
    d. most Native Americans refused to play traditional games on the reservations established by the U.S. government

20. In the author's comments about Oxendine's analysis of the history of sports among Native Americans, he notes that when we study the history of sports, we should
    a. check only official sources
    b. be careful to remember sequences of dates and events
    c. be aware of whose perspectives are being represented and whose are being ignored*
    d. remember that sports usually reflect the interests of the average working person in a culture

21. According to the description of today's high-profile, organized, competitive sports (as found in the boxed section), the sports played in most industrialized countries around the world
    a. transcend the secular world and offer participants experiences that are religious in nature
    b. involve a clear emphasis on setting and breaking records*
    c. are designed to discourage specialized skill development
    d. involve complex, irrational activities which make scores meaningless

22. According to the review presented by the author, sport participation during the early years of the Industrial Revolution was
   a. very high because people had a desperate need for distractions from work
   b. very low because physical skills were in short supply among the rapidly expanding middle classes
   c. very high because work and play were seen as equally important parts of community life
   d. very low because work and production were emphasized much more than leisure and recreation*

23. Sport participation among urban workers was relatively rare during the early days of the Industrial Revolution. The author notes that in the United States, this participation was often limited to
   a. dancing and physical movement activities done mostly by white women
   b. bowling and billiards played mostly by white men*
   c. track and field events played mostly by black men
   d. softball played mostly by black women

24. During the later years of the Industrial Revolution, sport activities became more and more organized. As this happened, sports in North America
   a. became less popular among the upper classes
   b. brought working class people and wealthy people together in clubs
   c. generally reinforced existing class distinctions in society*
   d. became more and more separated from the rest of what was happening in society

25. Around the turn of the century (1900) in the United States and parts of Europe, the meanings associated with sports and sport participation began to change significantly. Gradually, sports came to be seen as
   a. vehicles for breaking down national loyalties and creating international consciousness
   b. activities that interfered with a person's ability to work
   c. activities that interfered with a person's ability to do good works
   d. tools for changing behavior and shaping character*

26. According to the analysis in the chapter, those who organized sport programs for young males around the turn of the century in the U.S. were primarily interested in
   a. turning lower-class boys into competitive leaders
   b. teaching lower-class boys how to fit into upper-class activities
   c. turning overfeminized middle-class boys into assertive leaders*
   d. teaching boys from all backgrounds the importance of leisure in their lives

27. According to the analysis in the chapter, organized recreation programs for girls around the turn of the century generally emphasized the development of
    a. leadership skills
    b. domestic skills*
    c. physical strength and stamina
    d. competitiveness rather than good health

28. The author explains that sex-integrated sport programs were discouraged for teenage children because contact between boys and girls would
    a. lead to male-female friendships in which sex and reproduction would be unimportant*
    b. involve exploitation instead of fun
    c. discourage girls from forming relationships with other girls
    d. encourage boys to take too much of an interest in becoming husbands and fathers

29. Sport participation among African Americans in the late 19th century in the U.S.
    a. was practically nonexistent
    b. occurred only when blacks played with members of white ethnic groups
    c. gradually became integrated until the emergence of Jim Crow laws*
    d. was completely segregated by race

30. Sport participation among older people around the turn of the century in the U.S. was not encouraged as much as participation was encouraged among young people. This was due to the belief that older people were
    a. uninterested in health issues
    b. already very active in sports
    c. too competitive to play most sports safely
    d. physically unable to engage in strenuous activities*

31. According to the material in the chapter, it could be concluded that historical changes in sports have
    a. occurred in line with an evolutionary pattern
    b. been outgrowths of struggles between people with different interests and resources*
    c. gone hand-in-hand with the increasing corruption of sport
    d. corresponded to military developments in all societies

32. The author makes the point that sports during the 1920s in the U.S. were
    a. totally different than the sports of today
    b. similar to today's sports in terms of general organization and connection to U.S. culture*
    c. dependent on technology to an even greater extent than sports today
    d. not the scenes of any of the problems that affect sports today

33. Unlike sports prior to the 20th century, the high-profile, organized, competitive sports of today are often influenced by
    a.   religious organizations
    b.   the values of the people who participate in them
    c.   profit-making and commercial interests*
    d.   providing diversions for the masses

ESSAY QUESTIONS

1.   In the first section of the chapter, the author states that those with the strongest vested interests and the most power are the ones who will generally have the most impact on how sports are defined, organized, and played in a group or society. Pick two of the historical time periods discussed in the chapter and show how those with the most power had the most impact on sports during those periods. Give examples to support your argument.

2.   Throughout history, sports have generally been constructed in connection with the values and experiences of men. In what ways is this an accurate conclusion, and what are some examples of how people have challenged it through the years?

3.   During a discussion of the problems affecting sports in the 1990s, one of your friends says that everything would be okay if we could only make our sports just like the sports of the Greeks. He says that the Greeks had a "pure" form of sport in which participation was widespread and tied to individual development. Would you agree with him? Using the materials from the chapter, what would you say in response to his suggestion?

4.   During the days of the Roman Empire, sports were converted into a form of spectacle. Using the definition of spectacle given in Chapter 1 along with the description of Roman sport events in Chapter 3, show what is meant by this statement.

5.   The high-profile, organized, competitive sports of today are different than but not necessarily better than the sports of each of the previous historical periods discussed in the chapter. Pick one of the periods and compare the sports of that period with the dominant forms of sports of today. Emphasize both the similarities and the differences in your comparison.

6.   The instructor in your introductory sociology class says that there are more gender inequities in sports during the 1990s than at any other point in human history. You disagree with him and he asks you to back up your case with some good examples from history. What would you say in making your case?

7. Many people believe that sports have always been activities which build positive relationships between wealthy people and poor people. Would you agree or disagree with this statement after reading Chapter 3? Using material from the chapter and from your own experience, show why you would agree or disagree.

8. Someone in the physics department has just invented a time machine that can take people back into history. A male friend of yours is an athlete who wants to use the machine to take him back to some period during which he could play sports. He thinks he might like to go back to the Middle Ages. He comes to you for advice on what sports were like during that time. What would you tell him, and would you suggest that he pick some other period than the Middle Ages?

9. Joseph Oxendine's analysis of the history of Indian sports in North America indicates that it is important to understand who writes history and why it is written. Why is this important when considering the history of Indian sports?

10. Around the turn of the century (1880 - 1920) people started seeing sports as more than simply a set of enjoyable pastimes; instead, sports came to be seen as educational experiences. What caused this change in definitions and how did it affect the way sports were organized and promoted?

11. At the same time that organized sports became an important part of the social landscape in many industrializing countries during the late 19th and early 20th centuries, people began to make connections between sports and their ideas about character, masculinity and femininity, skin color and ethnicity, and age and disability. Explain these connections and how they may have had an impact on social relations in society as a whole.

12. Sports have always been the same, but they have changed significantly throughout human history. Can you make sense out of this statement? Use the material from the chapter to show that this statement accurately describes sport over the past 2500 years.

13. The description of high-profile, organized, competitive sports given in the chapter is helpful for purposes of analysis, but it does not accurately portray all the physical activities and sports that people play today. Using your experiences show how many popular physical activities do not fit the seven characteristics outlined in the chapter. Identify the differences as you describe the activities.

CHAPTER 4
SPORTS AND SOCIALIZATION:
who plays and what happens to them?

CHAPTER OUTLINE

I.   What is socialization?
      A.   A functionalist approach to socialization
      B.   A conflict theory approach to socialization
      C.   New approaches to socialization

II.   Becoming involved and staying involved in sports
      A.   Example 1: the process of becoming an elite athlete
      B.   Example 2: the process of being accepted as an athlete
      C.   Example 3: to participate or not to participate

III. Changing or ending sport participation
      A.   Example 1: burnout among young athletes
      B.   Example 2: getting out of sports and getting on with life

IV.   Being involved in sports: what happens
      (BOX: "Power and performance versus pleasure and participation: different sports, different experiences, different consequences")
      A.   "Sports build character": if it isn't true, why do people believe it?

V.   New approaches to sports and socialization
      A.   Real life experiences: sport stories from athletes
            1.   Example 1: the moral lessons of little league
            2.   Example 2: lessons in the locker room
            3.   Media stories about experiences
      B.   Social worlds: living in sports
            1.   Example 1: learning to be a hero
            2.   Example 2: realizing image isn't everything
            3.   Example 3: living in the shadow of a man's world
            4.   Example 4: surviving in a ghetto
            5.   Sport worlds portrayed in the media
      C.   Ideology: sports as sites for struggling over how we think and what we do
            1.   Research examples

VI.   What socialization research doesn't tell us

VII. Conclusion: who plays and what happens

MULTIPLE CHOICE QUESTIONS

1.   According to the definition used by the author in this chapter, socialization refers to
        a.   a process through which people are molded by society
        b.   what happens whenever people interact with each other
        c.   an interactive process through which people learn about themselves and make decisions about their lives*
        d.   a one-way process of learning whereby one generation passes knowledge to the next generation in a culture

2.   The definition of socialization used by the author is based on a combination of
        a.   critical and interactionist theories*
        b.   a functionalist approach and conflict theory
        c.   a functionalist approach and interactionist theories
        d.   conflict theory and critical theories

3.   Functionalists and conflict theorists both use
        a.   models of socialization that emphasize economic forces
        b.   an internalization model of socialization*
        c.   an interactionist model of socialization
        d.   a model of socialization that is sexist and elitist

4.   A functionalist approach to socialization focuses on three things (sets of variables). Which of the following is not one of those three things?
        a.   the people and social institutions that do the socializing
        b.   the characteristics of those being socialized
        c.   the specific outcomes of socialization
        d.   the decision-making processes used by those experiencing socialization*

5.   Conflict theorists who have studied socialization have generally focused on issues such as
        a.   how athletes are victimized by those who control the conditions of sport participation*
        b.   the characteristics of significant others in the socialization process
        c.   how sports serve general "system needs" in a society
        d.   the ways in which sport participation builds positive character in athletes

6.   The author notes that since the early 1980s, those who study sports and socialization have begun to use research methods that emphasize
        a.   measurable socialization outcomes experienced by athletes in recreational sports
        b.   qualitative data providing detailed descriptions of sport experiences*
        c.   statistical analysis of quantitative data
        d.   data collected through surveys and mailed questionnaires

7.   The author argues that becoming involved and staying involved in sports is the result of
      a.   a serious decision made by individuals at some point in their lives
      b.   the needs of the social system of which a person is a part
      c.   forces that exist outside a person and determine decisions about participation in sports and other activities
      d.   a continuing process of decision-making that occurs in connection with changing events in a person's life*

8.   Chris Stevenson did a study in which he collected stories from elite athletes about their sport experiences. Stevenson concluded that becoming an elite athlete involved primarily
      a.   a process of gaining access to money and equipment needed for training
      b.   a series of coincidental experiences that shaped a person's life from an early age
      c.   a process of support, commitment, interaction, and identity formation*
      d.   the influence of parents who control their child's life and isolate that child from other social relationships

9.   Peter Donnelly and Kevin Young used stories collected from rock climbers and rugby players to study the process of becoming an athlete. The data they collected led them to conclude that becoming an athlete involved primarily
      a.   a process of acquiring knowledge about a sport and developing a socially accepted identity as an athlete*
      b.   being sponsored by a person or corporation with power and influence
      c.   being recognized as a person with the money needed to buy equipment used in the sport
      d.   a process of taking so many risks in a sport that one becomes recognized by other athletes

10.   The in-depth interviews done by Anita White and Jay Coakley led them to conclude that sport participation among adolescents in England was mainly the result of
      a.   the policies and programs of the British Sports Council
      b.   the decisions made by young people as their lives and circumstances changed over time*
      c.   rapidly changing fads related to fitness and sports
      d.   decisions made by large groups of young people living in the same neighborhoods

11.   Becoming involved and staying involved in sports is grounded in a series of processes. Which of the following does *not* refer to one of the processes identified by the author?
      a.   attitude adjustment*
      b.   self-reflection
      c.   social support
      d.   identity formation

12. After reviewing dozens of studies the author makes a series of conclusions about the phenomenon of changing or ending sport participation. Which of the following is *not* one of those conclusions?
    a. dropping out of a sport is often done in connection with other changes or transitions in a person's life
    b. when people stop playing a particular sport, they seldom cut all ties with sports
    c. the decision to drop out of sports is sometimes made because of negative experiences in sports
    d. people drop out of sports primarily because they are victims of some form of exploitation in sports*

13. In Coakley's analysis of "burnout," it is pointed out that when top level young athletes drop out of a sport they usually do it because
    a. they are tired of making all the decisions that must be made in their sport careers
    b. their priorities have been distorted by many years of sport participation and competition
    c. they see sport participation as interfering with the development of desired identities and personal autonomy*
    d. they fear the discovery of new things about themselves and their abilities as they approach adulthood

14. When Konstantinos Koukouris interviewed former athletes in a number of sports, he discovered that decisions to end or change sport participation were primarily associated with
    a. being cut by a coach or sponsor who was critical of their skills
    b. the need to take responsibility for their own lives, get jobs, and support themselves*
    c. a sudden desire to cut all ties with sport and with the lifestyles associated with their sport participation
    d. a refusal to use the new forms of technology involved in training for competitions

15. The author suggests that the experience of ending a long career in sports is most likely to involve problems when the person ending a career lacks material resources to make the transition to another career and has no
    a. excuse for discontinuing sport participation
    b. awards or records that sustain sport memories
    c. close friends who remain active in sports
    d. identity apart from an identity as an athlete*

16. According to the author, the character logic that has been widely used in connection with sports
   a. rests on the belief that sports always involve character-building experiences*
   b. has been used to discourage children from playing organized sports until they are 12 years old
   c. is applicable primarily to girls and women rather than boys and men
   d. was rigorously tested by researchers through the first half of the 20th century

17. Past studies of socialization based on an internalization model have produced inconclusive and inconsistent findings. The author explains that this is due primarily to three faulty assumptions made by researchers. These faulty assumptions revolve around the belief that
   a. athletes automatically resist negative influence coming from win-oriented coaches
   b. all athletes have similar and unique experiences in sports that are unavailable through other activities*
   c. sport is similar to other leisure and extracurricular activities engaged in by young people
   d. character is usually formed by the time a person is 14 years old

18. Sport experiences vary depending on how sports are organized and played. According to the author, power and performance sports are the dominant sport form in many societies today. Which of the following is *not* a characteristic of power and performance sports as the author describes them?
   a. an important goal of participation is setting records
   b. excellence is proven through competitive success and doing what is necessary to win
   c. pushing human limits and dominating opponents is important
   d. technology is to be avoided so that achievement is based only on what the body can do by itself*

19. The author explains that some sports are best described as pleasure and participation sports. These sports tend to emphasize
   a. the importance of achievement and progress
   b. connections with other people and the environment*
   c. the notion of competing against others rather than with others
   d. the idea that pleasure depends on competitive success

20. The author argues that power and performance sports are dominant today primarily because they
   a. emphasize competition and validate the position and privilege of wealthy people in democratic societies*
   b. promote popular ideas about human evolution and progress
   c. enable powerful people to use their physical skills to dominate others
   d. are associated with beliefs about the need for progressive political action

21. The author argues that when sports and socialization is studied, researchers should remember that
    a.   sport is structured so that athletes automatically internalize the lessons emphasized by coaches
    b.   there is no automatic connection between sport participation and building character*
    c.   the meanings associated with sport participation are much the same from one sport experience to the next
    d.   sport participation produces similar socialization outcomes despite the social relationships that exist in sports

22. The author emphasizes that when people insist that sport participation builds character, they often forget that sport programs
    a.   attract people with certain characteristics*
    b.   are designed to teach people how to cheat
    c.   are set up so that most of the best athletes drop out of sports before they get to the college level
    d.   destroy the self-confidence of most participants

23. According to the author, the belief that sport builds character is maintained because people who hold the belief focus their attention on
    a.   men's sports but not women's sports
    b.   on recreational rather than competitive sport programs
    c.   athletes who are successful at the highest levels of competition*
    d.   young people in inner-city community programs

24. The author suggests that when people cling to the unquestioned belief that "sport builds character," they generally conclude that
    a.   deviance among athletes is to be expected
    b.   athletes should be role models*
    c.   athletes should be allowed to be deviant
    d.   nonathletes have serious character weaknesses

25. The author argues that those who maintain an unquestioned belief that sport builds character often think of "character" in a way that emphasizes
    a.   similarities between men and women
    b.   the need for changes in gender relations
    c.   traditional "manly" traits within a society*
    d.   sensitivity toward others as a quality needed for success

26. In the section on new approaches to sports and socialization, the author notes that sociologists and other social scientists are learning more about socialization through three types of research. Which of the following is not one of those three?
    a.   research on sports as explained through the voices of sport participants
    b.   research on the social worlds created around sports
    c.   research on sports as sites for the formation of ideology
    d.   research on how people learn about sports from significant others*

27. New approaches to sports and socialization have led an increasing number of people in the sociology of sport to see sports as
   a. physical experiences rather than social experiences
   b. sites for socialization experiences rather than causes of socialization outcomes*
   c. personal activities rather than social activities
   d. forms of careers rather than forms of leisure

28. When Gary Alan Fine studied little league baseball players, he found that the socialization experiences of the preteen boys who played in the league emphasized
   a. what it means to be a man in U.S. culture*
   b. masculinity in terms of sensitivity and nurturance
   c. a general respect for girls their age
   d. a special disdain for boys who were older and stronger than they were

29. When Nancy Theberge studied a top-level women's ice hockey team in Canada, she found that the locker room was an important place for team bonding. She notes that locker room interaction involved
   a. hostile remarks about sex and sexuality
   b. jokes and degrading talk about men and relationships with men
   c. controlled forms of expression through which feelings were often hidden
   d. talk that gave meaning to the experience of playing hockey*

30. In the discussion of examples of new approaches to sports and socialization, the author notes that journalistic accounts of sport experiences are
   a. not useful unless the journalists have had extensive training in sociology
   b. useful if they are read critically*
   c. usually better than studies done by sociologists
   d. generally combinations of fact and fiction

30. The author uses the term "social world" to refer to
   a. a special place that people go to enjoy being with other people
   b. a set of relationships that have a strong social character
   c. a way of life and a mindset that develop around a particular activity and the people involved in it*
   d. a media-generated set of images and meanings that shape how people think and act

31. When Patti and Peter Adler studied a big-time intercollegiate men's basketball team, they discovered that team members gradually
   a. experienced a form of burnout that ended the careers of half of the entire team
   b. became so engulfed in doing their coursework and playing basketball that they ignored their social lives
   c. developed a strong dislike of their coaches and team practices
   d. became so committed to basketball that they viewed the rest of the world in terms of their identities as athletes*

32. In his study of elite competitive bodybuilding in California, Alan Klein observed that male bodybuilders
   a. tended to be insecure about their masculinity*
   b. had a multidimensional view of themselves and their abilities
   c. often presented themselves in public as homosexuals
   d. had high levels of self-esteem, even when they received little attention and approval from others

33. When Todd Crosset studied the LPGA, he found that the players emphasized what he called an "ethic of prowess." This ethic was formed partly in response to
   a. the psychological intimidation that all the golfers used to obtain a competitive edge
   b. the tough golf courses on which they had to play their tournaments
   c. the potentially negative effects of how some people defined gender and viewed women athletes*
   d. the demands placed on the golfers' lives by husbands and children

34. The author explains that some sociologists are beginning to study socialization as a community and cultural process. The research of these sociologists tends to focus on
   a. the relationships between athletes and leaders in community politics
   b. sports as sites for creating and learning the stories that people use for making sense out of their lives*
   c. sports as meaningless forms of art and entertainment in the community
   d. why sports have similar consequences across all communities and cultures

35. Research on sports and socialization as a community and cultural process is partly inspired by the ideas of Antonio Gramsci. Using Gramsci's ideas, sociologists have identified sports as important in connection with socialization because sports are
   a. activities that people can do by themselves or with others
   b. shaped by system needs in society
   c. popular forms of pleasure in people's lives*
   d. forms of physical labor

36. According to a Gramscian analysis of sports and society, sports are important social phenomena because they are
   a. vehicles for creating disagreement and social conflict in society
   b. mechanisms for promoting democracy and the interests of citizens in society
   c. activities that distract attention away from issues of ideology
   d. contexts through which ideological messages can be presented to people*

37. The author explains that many sociologists see sports as important because sports are involved in hegemonic processes in society. Hegemony refers to a social process through which
   a. ideologies that favor the interests of those with power in society become dominant in society as a whole*
   b. privileged people in society share their resources and power with others in the society
   c. people identify system needs in a society and then work to satisfy those needs
   d. class-based forms of social conflict become intense and disruptive in society

38. Using one of the new approaches to socialization, David Andrews studied the "persona" created in connection with Michael Jordan. He concludes that through media images of Jordan, the Jordan persona was
   a. used to raise questions about race and gender in society
   b. tied to the legacies of colonialism and racism around the world
   c. severed from African American experiences and culture*
   d. cleverly linked with inner-city, minority lifestyles

39. In his discussion of research needed in the future, the author says that we need studies of how the language used in certain sports influences sport participation decisions. He notes that the "language of sports" in many schools is
   a. based on traditional masculine images and orientations*
   b. shaped by the interests of cheerleaders and teachers
   c. carefully controlled to promote gender equity in sports
   d. grounded in the values and experiences of all students

ESSAY QUESTIONS

1. One of your friends says that when she has a child she will make sure that her son or daughter is active in sports because sport participation teaches certain important lessons. You tell her that socialization involves complex interactional processes and is not just a matter of internalizing the messages and experiences shaped by parents. She does not understand what you are saying, so you give her a definition of socialization and examples of what it means. Write an essay in which you outline your explanation of the socialization process and how it occurs in connection with sports.

2. "Becoming involved in sports is as much an issue of identity development as it is an issue of skill development." Using research reviewed in the first section of the chapter, explain what this statement means, and use your own experience (or the experiences of your friends) to give examples either supporting or contradicting the research.

3.   Throughout a person's life, sport participation patterns change. Use your own life and the lives of one of your parents to identify some of those changes, and then explain what factors influenced your decisions and your parent's decisions about sport participation through your lives. You may have to interview one of your parents (or another adult about the same age as your parent) to write this essay. Use material in the chapter to organize your interview and your essay.

4.   A recent story in your local newspaper reported that there is a relatively high dropout rate in youth sports in your city/town. In a Letter to the Editor commenting on the story, a local resident says that the dropout rate is high because young people today are lazy and unwilling to make commitments. You write a responding letter to the editor in which you outline all the reasons why dropout rates in many youth sports are relatively high.

5.   You have just done a literature review of the topic "sports and character development." After reading 10 studies, you are confused by the conflicting findings: some studies show that sport participation is associated with positive character development, while others show the opposite or no association at all between participation and character development. In your report, it is up to you to explain these confusing findings. Use the material in the chapter to outline your explanation.

6.   The consequences of sport participation are likely to vary with a number of factors, including the types of sports a person plays. Explain how sport experiences can vary depending on whether a person in playing in a power and performance sport as opposed to a pleasure and participation sport.

7.   The author explains the major differences between power and performance sports and pleasure and participation sports. However, many sports actually consist of combination of these two types of sports. Use your own experience to illustrate that real-life sports cannot be neatly divided into two distinct and different types.

8.   The author argues that certain sport forms become dominant in a society because they "reproduce the privilege of powerful people in the society." He then goes on to say that this is why power and performance sports are dominant in many societies around the world today. Explain what he means, and then indicate whether you agree or disagree with his argument.

9.   In the U.S., there is a strong emphasis on the competitive dimensions of sports. The emphasis on competition is probably greater in U.S. sports than in the sports in most other countries. A person who has read the writings of Antonio Gramsci and other critical theorists suggests that this is because the U.S. is a democratic society that has more socio-economic inequality than other societies, and that competitive sports can be used to justify inequality in many people's minds. Explain how someone could make such a statement and indicate whether you agree or disagree with it.

10. Wealthy and powerful people in many western societies have sponsored organized, competitive sports; in fact, they have given billions of dollars every year to make sure these sports are publicized, promoted, and played for spectators around the world. This is interesting because many of these sports do not make money for sponsors. So why do wealthy and powerful people continue to sponsor sports rather than using their money in other ways?

11. A coach of a high school all-star basketball team tells you that after working with the players on her team, she thinks that sport competition definitely builds character. You tell her she should be careful when making such a general conclusion. She tells you that she has personal experience to back up her conclusion. Explain why the coach, like many others in your community, clings to her belief that competition builds character.

12. One of your female friends strongly believes that sport builds character. When you hear this, you tell her that such a belief often works to the disadvantage of women in society. She thinks you are crazy, and she demands an explanation of why you think this. How would you explain your statement to her?

13. The author argues that sports are *sites* for socialization experiences rather than *causes* of socialization outcomes. He uses three examples from research and the media to illustrate what this means. Choose one of those examples and show how and why sports are more accurately viewed as sites for socialization experiences than as causes of socialization outcomes.

14. It is difficult to understand the socialization experiences of athletes unless you have an understanding of the social world in which an athlete plays a sport. Use at least two examples from the chapter (Division I intercollegiate men's basketball, competitive bodybuilding, the LPGA, and/or world class women's gymnastics) to illustrate this point.

15. Many people see socialization only as a personal experience, but social scientists are now doing research showing that socialization is a community and cultural process that emphasizes images and messages going beyond the experiences of individual athletes. Use at least two examples from the chapter to illustrate the ways that sports involve processes of community and cultural socialization.

16. You are writing a grant to fund research on sports and socialization. After reading the chapter, you have decided that there is a real need to do research on two particular topics or issues. Which topics have you chosen to include in your grant proposal? Explain why research on these topics is needed, and how your findings might be used to extend our knowledge of sports and socialization.

CHAPTER 5
SPORTS AND CHILDREN:
are organized programs worth the effort?

CHAPTER OUTLINE

I.   The origin and development of organized youth sports
        A.   Organized sports and changes in the family

II.   Major trends in youth sports today
        (BOX: "Organized sports and the goals of sponsors: how do politics affect sport participation?")
        A.   The privatization of youth sports
        B.   Emphasis on the "performance principle"

III.   Different experiences: informal player-controlled sports versus organized adult-controlled sports
        A.   Informal, player-controlled sports
                1.   A word of caution
        B.   Formal, adult-controlled sports
        C.   Analysis of differences

IV.   Three questions about youth sports
        A.   When are children ready to play sports?
                1.   Answer 1: it's never too early for physical play
                2.   Answer 2: any child in school is ready for organized physical activities
                3.   Answer 3: organized sports before age 8 and competition before age 12 must be matched with children's needs and abilities
                4.   A look back at the original question
        B.   Do boys and girls play sports differently?
        (BOX: "Gender differences versus experiences: what should we study?")

V.   Recommendations for changing children's sports
        A.   Changing informal sports
        B.   Changing organized sports
                1.   Increasing action
                        a.   Recommendations
                2.   Increasing personal involvement
                        a.   Recommendations
                3.   Creating close scores
                        a.   Recommendations
                4.   Maintaining relationships
                        a.   Recommendations

VI.   Prospects for change
      A.   Coaching education as a means of producing changes

VII. Conclusion: are organized youth sport programs worth the effort?

MULTIPLE CHOICE QUESTIONS

1.   Organized youth sports were originally developed to teach lower-class boys how
     to work together peacefully and to help middle-class boys
     a.   counteract the influence of home lives dominated by women*
     b.   become less competitive
     c.   accept the fact that they would not be as successful as their fathers
     d.   learn homemaking skills they could use after they got married

2.   According to data collected in the United States, the majority of parents
     a.   discourage their children from playing organized sports because there is
          not enough emphasis put on development
     b.   encourage their children to play organized sports because of the heavy
          emphasis put on winning in the programs
     c.   encourage their children to play organized sports but think that many
          organized sports place too much emphasis on winning*
     d.   discourage their children from playing organized sports because of a fear
          of injuries

3.   The author argues that more children than ever are in organized sports at least
     partly because of changes that have occurred recently in families. Which of the
     following is *not* among the family changes that have encouraged participation in
     organized youth sports?
     a.   many parents today see the world as a dangerous place for their children
     b.   the expectations for parents today are more demanding than they have
          been in the past
     c.   the number of families with both parents working outside the home is
          very high today
     d.   more parents want their children to learn how to play informal games
          without adult supervision*

4.   According to the author, one downside of new expectations for parents to keep
     their children in organized and adult-controlled activities is that
     a.   too many new parks and open spaces have been provided in urban areas
     b.   participation in these activities creates rebelliousness in children
     c.   people without resources may be defined as failures as parents*
     d.   parents get to know their children too well

5. According to the author's analysis, the trend toward privatization in organized youth sports has
   a. made youth programs more selective and exclusive*
   b. the most adverse affect on people from upper-income areas where public programs were most common
   c. been especially helpful for single parents who need good programs for their children
   d. created many new youth programs that are racially integrated

6. On the basis of material in the chapter, it could be concluded that an emphasis on the performance principle is most likely to be found in organized youth sports programs that are funded by
   a. public, tax-supported recreation organizations
   b. public non-profit community organizations
   c. private non-profit sport organizations
   d. private commercial clubs*

7. In organized youth sport programs that emphasize the performance principle, the author hypothesizes that there will be a greater emphasis on
   a. parents to ignore the sport development of their children
   b. using irrational criteria for assessing children's sport experiences
   c. sport specialization among children*
   d. pressuring children to try as many different sports as possible

8. The author is very critical of high-performance sport programs for young children. He argues that in some of these programs
   a. young athletes become similar to child laborers and they may need the protection of child labor laws*
   b. the parents and coaches use secret training methods previously used in youth programs in communist countries
   c. children are encouraged to quit when they have injuries
   d. the child athletes rebel against coaches and take over their own training

9. According to the author, one of the indicators that some children reject highly structured sport programs emphasizing the performance principle is
   a. increased dropout rates in all organized activities, even including school
   b. the growth and popularity of informal, "alternative" sports*
   c. a recent increase in violent crime among young people
   d. the high turnover among coaches in those programs

10. According to research done by the author and his students, the informal, player-controlled sports played by children tend to emphasize four things. Which of the following is *not* one of those things?
    a. action
    b. close scores
    c. opportunities to reaffirm friendships
    d. equal treatment for all players*

11. In informal, player-controlled sports, children seek personal involvement. Personal involvement in informal games is often promoted by the use of
    a. numerous substitutes and second-string players
    b. unique game rules and handicap systems*
    c. adult supervisors
    d. large playing areas and large teams

12. According to data collected by the author, deviance in informal player-controlled sports is most serious when it involves
    a. disobeying team captains
    b. lack of knowledge of complex rules
    c. joking around
    d. a disruption of action*

13. The author notes that generalizations about informal sports among children are difficult to make. He explains that the dynamics of these sports often vary depending on
    a. the social class of the players
    b. the availability of play spaces and equipment*
    c. the size and strength of the best players
    d. the personalities of the players

14. According to the author's study, formal, adult-controlled sports usually have an emphasis on
    a. action and involvement
    b. rules and positions*
    c. freedom and expression
    d. letting players solve their own arguments

15. In the description of formal, adult-controlled sports contained in the chapter, it is noted that children in these sports
    a. are most disappointed when they don't get enough playing time*
    b. are all obsessed with winning games, championships, and personal awards
    c. usually become visibly upset when referees' calls cause breaks in the action
    d. have frequent arguments over rules and rules interpretations

16. After reading Chapter 5, which of the following would you expect to observe if you attended both an organized Little League baseball game and a pickup stickball game in a vacant lot?
    a. there would be fewer strikeouts in the Little League game
    b. team scores in the pickup game would be higher*
    c. unique playing styles would be seen more often in the Little League game
    d. game rules would be applied to all players equally in the pickup game

17. In comparing player experiences in informal games and formal games, what is more likely to be learned through the experiences in formal games?
    a. interpersonal skills
    b. how to enforce rules
    c. decision-making skills
    d. knowledge of game rules*

18. After doing a five-year study of children's after-school activities (summarized in the chapter), Patricia and Peter Adler suggest that extensive participation in adult-organized activities such as youth sports may prepare children
    a. to reject adult models of work and achievement
    b. to organizing their own activities and making compromises in their relationships with peers
    c. for passively accepting the adult world as given and unchangeable*
    d. to live longer, healthier lives governed by strict rules

19. An overall comparison of informal games and formal games led the author to conclude that
    a. informal games are action-centered while formal games are rule-centered*
    b. both informal games and formal games are rule-centered
    c. informal games are player-centered and the formal games are action-centered
    d. neither informal games nor formal games are action-centered

20. The author gives a series of answers to the question, "When are children ready to play sports?" Which of the following is *not* one of those answers?
    a. it's never too early for physical play
    b. organized sports before age eight and competition before age 12 must be matched with children's needs and abilities
    c. playing organized sports before age six is only advised when the child shows signs of real ability*
    d. any child in school is ready for organized physical activities

21. The author argues that one of the possible dangers of early involvement in physical activities is that in a culture such as U.S. culture, the physical play of children may
    a. emphasize performance and goal achievement over expression*
    b. random movements rather than systematic practice until the child does it right
    c. distract children from the goals of trying to be perfect in what they do
    d. create delayed balance and coordination problems that appear during early adulthood

22. After reading the author's analysis, what qualities would you look for in the staff of an organized physical activity program that your five-year-old child might participate in? The staff should be
   a. trained in the rules of organized sports so they know what team positions are best suited to a child's abilities
   b. familiar with how to involve children into competitive activities so they experience both success and failure
   c. highly organized and quick to control children when there is too much experimentation with movement
   d. ready to listen to children and willing to allow them freedom to use their bodies on their own terms*

23. According to the author, eight-year-old children on organized soccer teams play "beehive soccer" because
   a. their coaches teach it as a form of strategy
   b. they feel insecure when they are not close to their teammates
   c. they do not have the cognitive abilities to understand team strategy and structure*
   d. parents tell them that they have to be close to the ball in order to score

24. The author explains that there are two ways to avoid the "beehive soccer" phenomenon with children under 12 years old. One is to alter the games and the other is to systematically condition children to do what they must do to play the game correctly. According to the author, using the second tactic
   a. is always advisable unless coaches are trained in physical education
   b. often destroys much of the action and personal involvement that children enjoy*
   c. works more often with boys than with girls
   d. is better in the long run because it shows children that games should not be changed under any circumstances

25. The author argues that in sport programs for children under the age of 12, there should be an emphasis on cooperation and confidence because
   a. self-confidence enables children to take physical risks that will make them tough in the long run
   b. self-confident and cooperative children are able to quickly learn deceptive strategies used in competitive games
   c. if children have not learned to cooperate, competitive games can be nasty and brutish*
   d. the secret to success in real sports is being able to cooperate without being friendly with others

26. The author notes that a child's sport participation frequently brings parents and children together in positive ways. However, he suggests that family relationships may be damaged when
    a. children come to believe that parental attention depends on playing sports and being good at it*
    b. parents are not willing to spend money on equipment and uniforms
    c. children focus more on their relationships with parents than on developing necessary sport skills
    d. parents have more than two children playing in different sports during different seasons

27. Research indicates that patterns of playing sports are in some ways different for girls than they are for boys. According to the author, these differences are related to
    a. experiences shared by all girls and experiences shared by all boys as they grow up
    b. hormones that dictate a person's level of aggression under conditions of competition
    c. sex differences in the shoulder structures of males and females
    d. how the meanings of gender influence the experiences that boys and girls have while growing up*

28. In the special boxed section on "Gender differences versus experience," the author argues that gender-difference questions are loaded because
    a. girls will seldom answer any questions related to gender differences
    b. they can lead researchers to ignore variations in experiences and behaviors*
    c. everyone already knows that males and females will always be different
    d. men do most of the research on sport, and they don't know much about the unique experiences of girls

29. The author notes that there are many childhood experiences that influence physical activity patterns among boys and girls. Which of the following childhood experiences is not mentioned by the author as this issue is discussed?
    a. boys learn to see themselves as more physically skilled than girls, even when they aren't
    b. boys mature more slowly than girls, so they develop more coordination than girls do*
    c. some physical education teachers, especially in the past, have had different expectations for girls than for boys
    d. girls learn to minimize the physical space they occupy, while boys learn to claim space around them

50

30. The author recommends that when it comes to informal, child-controlled sports, the goals of adults should be to learn from them and
    a. enable children to play them as safely as possible*
    b. join in them so children can learn from adults
    c. help children get more organized so they more closely resemble real sports
    d. force their children to play them every day

31. What is the major source of information used by the author when he makes recommendations for changes in organized youth sport programs?
    a. the informal games of children themselves*
    b. child psychology experts in the U.S. and Europe
    c. research on the meaning of play in industrial societies
    d. principles used in the field of business management

32. The general recommendations for changing organized youth sport programs given in the chapter are related to four different goals. Which of the following is *not* one of those goals?
    a. creating close scores in games
    b. maintaining relationships between players
    c. creating the skills needed to play elite sports*
    d. increasing personal involvement among participants

33. In the specific recommendations for change made in the chapter, which of the following was *not* included?
    a. use handicap systems to keep game scores close
    b. rotate players between positions to increase the range of their experiences
    c. increase action and scoring opportunities
    d. add more referees and umpires to control action in games*

34. When the author discusses changes needed in high performance sport programs for children, he supports a radical idea that has been suggested by others. This idea is that
    a. television and media coverage ought to be banned from all youth sports
    b. parents should not be allowed to travel with their children who participate in elite competitions
    c. new child labor laws ought to be applied to elite youth sports*
    d. revenues generated by events involving elite child athletes be donated to a medical fund to be used by those athletes

35. In the author's discussion of "prospects for change" in youth sports, he predicts that changes will be slow because
    a. many adults have vested interests in keeping youth sports as they are*
    b. there is a growing number of facilities and fields for youth sports
    c. people who run sport programs come from ethnic backgrounds where maintaining tradition is more important than change
    d. burnout rates are so high that people are afraid to make any changes

36. According to the author, coaching education programs offer hope for bringing about needed changes in organized youth sports. However, the author worries that coaching education programs may ultimately
    a. lead adults to emphasize child development over sport development
    b. lead to too many structural changes in youth sports
    c. encourage coaches to ignore technoscience information that can be used to improve children's sport skills
    d. turn coaches into sports efficiency experts rather than teachers of young people*

37. According to the conclusion at the close of the chapter, organized sport programs for children are worth the effort when the adults control the programs
    a. put the interests of children ahead of the organizational needs of the programs
    b. try to keep the programs highly organized so children know what to expect and how to act
    c. do a good job of preparing children to play at higher levels of competition
    d. treat the children like little adults and show them what adult life is all about*

ESSAY QUESTIONS

1. The growth and popularity of organized youth sports is related to general changes in society and in the ways families are defined and organized. What characteristics of culture and family life today are associated with the current popularity of organized youth sports? In addition to using material from the text, use examples from your own experience or the experiences of your friends to illustrate these characteristics. (Note to Instructor: If you are teaching at a campus where students have access to members of their own families, ask students to interview a family member over the age of 45 and ask what youth sports were like when their older relative was growing up.)

2. One of your father's friends is known for his arguments against taxes. He frequently calls for an elimination of tax-supported programs. When he discovers you are taking a sociology of sport course, he says that he thinks all youth sport programs should be privatized and organized to emphasize the development of athletic excellence. Would you agree or disagree with him? Use material in the text and your own experience to support your position.

3. If you were watching an informal, player-controlled game among a group of nine to 12-year-olds in a vacant lot, what would you expect to see? What are children interested in when they create and play games on their own? Give examples to illustrate your points.

4.   When informal games were compared with formal games in the chapter, it was said that informal games are action-centered and formal games are rule-centered. What does this mean and what are the implications of this statement for the experiences of those who participate in these two types of games?

5.   Your younger sister is on an organized soccer team for eight-year-olds. At the first game, you notice that the coaches and most of the parents are on the sidelines yelling at your sister and her teammates to "stay in position." The game continues and the players remain out of position no matter what is yelled from the sidelines. Your parents are disappointed in your sister's first performance in a game. They think that the coaches are incompetent and that girls just can't play team sports. What would you say to your parents? How would you explain the fact that your sister's team looked disorganized during the game?

6.   In your sociology of the family class, the instructor says that organized youth sport programs are good because they bring families together in a common activity. You have an opportunity during the discussion to qualify this statement by your instructor. What would you say? Do youth sports bring families together? Are the results of this coming together always good? When are problems most likely to occur?

7.   You are a member of city council in a large eastern city. Many of the children in your district play street ball during the warm months of the year. One of the council members suggests a rule banning street ball because it is a dangerous, worthless activity that interferes with the traffic patterns in the city. You are interested in the safety of the young people in your district, but you also want to come to their defense and show that street ball is not a useless activity. What would you say to the council about street ball, and what kinds of policy suggestions might you make in this situation?

8.   You are the physical education teacher in an experimental school that accepts pre-school-age children as young as three and elementary school-age children through grade 6 (about 12 years old). Using material from the text, explain how you would organize the physical activity and sport programs at the school. How would the programs change for children of different ages?

9.   Your brother and sister-in-law are the parents of two children. One is five and the other is eight. They want their children to be involved in physical activities and sports. They ask you for advice because they know you are taking a sociology of sport course. Explain what you would say to them as you advise them about when their children should be involved in certain kinds of programs and how that involvement might affect parent-child relationships.

10.   Your brother and sister-in-law have a new baby daughter whom they want to be active in sports as she grows up. After reading the material on the differences between the informal games of boys and girls and some of the reasons why these differences exist, what advice would you have for these new parents?

11. You are visiting your sister and brother-in-law. They have a baby daughter whom they treat in an overprotective manner. They worry about her physical safety and they don't let her out of their sight for long. They give her dolls to play with and put her in a dress and tights every day so she will "learn to be a lady when she grows up." Will she grow up playing different kinds of games than the ones played by her brother who is three years older than she is? How will her games be different?

12. If you are a man, interview two women your age, or if you are a woman, interview two men your age, and ask them to describe their experiences in physical activities and sports during their childhood and early adolescence (ages six - 15). Compare their experiences to your own and explain why there are similarities and differences in the ways you played while growing up. What are the key factors that seem to promote or inhibit involvement in physical activities and/or sports?

13. As a new member of the park and recreation department you have been put in charge of reorganizing one of the youth sport programs in the district. You are told you have complete freedom to do anything you want. The first thing you do is call a meeting of all coaches and parents. What would you say in your presentation to them? You want to change the program so it meets the needs and interests of the children involved.

14. As a grade-school basketball coach working with 4th graders, it is your job to create a basketball program for your school and three other schools in your league. When you go to your first meeting with the three other coaches, what kinds of suggestions would you make for changes in your existing program (which is very similar to the program at the local high school)?

15. Coaching education programs are seen by some people as a sure way to improve organized sport programs for children. You are working for a Parks and Recreation Department in a large city, and you have been asked to outline the features of a coaching education program that will bring about needed changes in youth sports. Discuss what issues you consider to be important as you put together the outline.

16. After reading this chapter on organized sport programs for children, one of your classmates becomes discouraged and says the programs are just not worth all the effort adults put into them. You disagree and say they are worth the effort. How would you support your position in the discussion?

CHAPTER 6
DEVIANCE IN SPORTS:
is it getting out of control?

CHAPTER OUTLINE

I. Problems faced when studying deviance in sports

II. Defining and studying deviance in sports: three approaches
   - A. The absolutist approach: "It's either right or wrong"
   - B. The relativist approach: "It all depends on who makes the rules"
   - C. An alternative approach: "Deviance can be negative or positive"
     1. Research on positive deviance
     2. The "sport ethic" and deviance in sports
   (BOX: "Just do it: the sport ethic and Nike ads")
     3. Who is most likely to engage in positive deviance?
     4. Positive deviance and group dynamics
     5. Controlling positive deviance in sports

III. Research on deviance among athletes
   - A. On-the-field and sport-related deviance
   - B. Off-the-field, away-from-sport deviance
     1. Delinquency rates
     2. Academic cheating
     3. Alcohol use and binge drinking
     4. Sexual assault
   - C. Why focus only on deviance among athletes?
   (BOX: "Is sport participation a 'cure' for deviant behavior?")

IV. Performance-enhancing substances: a study of positive deviance in sports
   - A. History and causes of substance use among athletes
   - B. Defining, identifying, and banning performance-enhancing drugs
   - C. Drug testing in sports
     1. Background and history
     2. Testing as a deterrent
   - D. Controlling substance use in sports

V. Conclusion: is deviance in sports out of control?

MULTIPLE CHOICE QUESTIONS

1. In the introduction to the chapter, the author notes that highly publicized cases of deviance among athletes, coaches, and others in sports have shocked and disillusioned many people primarily because
    a. the rates of deviance in the rest of society are so low
    b. athletes in the past have seldom engaged in any deviant behavior
    c. many of the perpetrators of deviance are women athletes and coaches
    d. people believe that sport participation is a character-building experience*

2. The author explains that studying deviance in sports presents unique problems primarily because
    a. psychological research shows that athletes have conforming personalities
    b. coaches enforce rules so strictly that deviance seldom occurs
    c. what is normal in sports may be deviant outside sports*
    d. athletes have enough money to hire good lawyers and avoid prosecution for deviance

3. According to the author, one of the specific problems faced when studying deviance in sports is that much of the deviance involves behavior grounded in
    a. overconformity and overacceptance of norms and expectations in sports*
    b. a rejection of norms and expectations in society and sports
    c. strong feelings of despair and alienation among athletes and coaches
    d. a strong desire on the part of athletes to avoid responsibility

4. According to the author, one of the three specific problems faced when studying deviance in sports is that athletic training today
    a. is done in settings where athletes are difficult to observe
    b. uses science and medicine to the point that training methods challenge ideas about what is normal and what isn't*
    c. is controlled strictly by coaches and sponsors, not athletes
    d. is based on methods that have been used in exactly the same ways for at least a century

5. When people use an "absolutist" approach to studying deviance, they identify as deviant any behavior in sports that
    a. leads another person to be injured
    b. does not fit with what they define as the "ideals" of sport*
    c. violates the expectations of "moral" people in society
    d. does not contribute to winning or the enhancement of performance

6. The use of an "absolutist" approach to studying deviance in sports would be most common among
    a. critical theorists, but not feminists
    b. conflict theorists
    c. feminists, but not other critical theorists
    d. functionalists*

7. According to an "absolutist" approach, those who violate rules in society usually do so because
    a. they are victims of exploitation
    b. they are rebelling against a lack of freedom
    c. they lack moral character*
    d. the rules themselves are unfair or biased

8. Those using an "absolutist" approach are likely to recommend that deviance in sports is best controlled through
    a. changing the rules
    b. redistributing power within sport
    c. giving athletes more responsibility
    d. using more effective methods of social control*

9. According to a "relativist" approach to studying deviance in sports, all deviant behavior is an outgrowth of
    a. a labeling process through which certain behaviors are defined as deviant by those with power*
    b. a breakdown in the socialization process within sports
    c. the uncontrolled desire among athletes to be "number one"
    d. a basic weakness in human nature

10. Sociologists most likely to use a "relativist" approach are
    a. critical theorists, including feminists
    b. conflict theorists*
    c. feminists, but not other critical theorists
    d. functionalists

11. Those using a "relativist" approach often assume that deviance in sports could be controlled if
    a. athletes were socialized more efficiently
    b. everyone in sports was responsible for the actions of everyone else, and not just themselves
    c. formal competition in sports was eliminated
    d. dehumanizing political and economic systems were changed*

12. According to the author, deviance in sports is best understood if it is seen as
    a. a result of biased and coercive rules
    b. involving either underconformity or overconformity*
    c. involving moral irresponsibility and failure
    d. the result of attempts to exploit other people for personal gain

13. The author favors a third approach to studying deviance in sports, one described as a "critical normal distribution" approach. This approach requires that a distinction be made between people whose behavior is motivated by
    a. a lack of concern about norms vs overacceptance of norms among athletes*
    b. a lack of moral character vs commitment to morals among athletes
    c. an insensitivity to others vs real concern for others among athletes
    d. a lack of commitment to the integrity of sports vs deep respect for sports among athletes

14. According to the "critical normal distribution" approach, there are two forms of deviance: negative deviance and positive deviance. The author explains that
    a. positive deviance is harmless while negative deviance is dangerous
    b. negative deviance in sports is so rare that sociologists have ignored it in the past
    c. too much positive deviance will lead to anarchy
    d. both forms of deviance are dangerous although positive deviance is often more difficult to control*

15. After reviewing research on positive deviance, the author explains that using a "critical normal distribution" approach to study and understand this form of deviance requires that sociologists
    a. study child athletes rather than adult athletes
    b. avoid studying athletes in sports where there are high injury rates
    c. critically examine the value systems that exist in sports*
    d. look for personality defects in athletes who regularly overconform to the norms in sports

16. The author explains that understanding deviance in sports requires an understanding of "the sport ethic." Which of the following beliefs is *not* one of the core beliefs in the sport ethic?
    a. an athlete strives for distinction
    b. an athlete accepts no limits in the pursuit of possibilities
    c. an athlete accepts risks except when injuries are likely*
    d. an athlete makes sacrifices for "the game"

17. The author argues that the sport ethic becomes dangerous and a source of deviance in sports when
    a. athletes raise too many questions about its meaning
    b. people in sports do not draw lines to determine how far they will go in following the norms of the ethic*
    c. when athletes reject the norms of the sport ethic and make up their own rules
    d. referees and umpires do not take the sport ethic seriously when they enforce rules

58

18. In the author's discussion of a 1996 Nike ad (in a boxed section) run during the Olympics, he hypothesizes that the ad
    a. discouraged both positive and negative deviance
    b. discouraged negative deviance
    c. condoned and encouraged positive deviance*
    d. contradicted the norms of the sport ethic

19. According to the author, one of the general reasons athletes may overconform to the sport ethic is because they
    a. love their sports and they want to continue playing*
    b. were pressured by their parents to play sports
    c. want to be seen as normal by people outside of sports
    d. want to be different than their fellow athletes

20. Not all athletes are equally likely to overconform to the sport ethic. The author suggests that the athletes most likely to do so are those who see achievement as their only way to get ahead and those who have
    a. identities grounded in what they do outside of sports
    b. agents who give them bad advice
    c. a high physical tolerance for pain
    d. low self-esteem and are eager to make sacrifices to be accepted by fellow athletes*

21. The author suggests that rates of positive deviance would be highest on teams where coaches
    a. emphasize responsibility and decision making among athletes
    b. create environments that keep athletes in a perpetual state of adolescence*
    c. encourage athletes to ask questions about how sport participation is connected to the rest of their lives
    d. emphasize conditioning and learning basic tactics and techniques

22. The author argues that when athletes collectively overconform to the norms of the sport ethic, they sometimes develop a sense of arrogance or *hubris* that leads them to see themselves as separate from and superior to the rest of the community. The author hypothesizes that this hubris
    a. provides a strong incentive to do community service
    b. creates group dynamics that may encourage dangerous forms of negative deviance*
    c. destroys the ability of teams to work together in supportive ways
    d. discourages all negative forms of deviance on and off the field

23. According to the author's explanation, much of the positive deviance in sports is due to an athlete's desire to
    a. win
    b. make money
    c. play and be accepted as an athlete by peers in sport*
    d. avoid media coverage and excessive attention from fans

24. According to the author, finding ways to control "positive deviance" in sports requires a close examination of the
    a.   backgrounds of athletes, coaches, and spectators
    b.   economics of sport
    c.   moral characters of athletes and coaches
    d.   meaning and organization of sports*

25. Controlling "positive deviance" in sports presents a unique challenge because
    a.   people in sports never learn to follow rules
    b.   people in many societies no longer respect any types of rules
    c.   those who enforce rules in sports have mixed feelings about controlling "positive deviance"*
    d.   coaches feel uncomfortable discussing rules for athletes

26. From what research tells us about on-the-field deviance among athletes, it can be concluded that behaviors such as cheating, "dirty play," and shaving points are
    a.   definitely more common today than in the past
    b.   probably less common today than in the past*
    c.   only found in heavy contact sports
    d.   nonexistent among today's athletes

27. The author suggests that athletes today seem to engage in more sport-related forms of deviance than athletes in the past because
    a.   coaches today are less concerned about control than they were in the past
    b.   society is less orderly today than in the past
    c.   sports and sport organizations today have more rules than they have had in the past*
    d.   rules in sports are enforced more strictly today than in the past

28. Research findings on sport participation and general delinquency rates generally show that delinquency rates among student-athletes
    a.   are often lower than rates for other students from similar backgrounds*
    b.   are always higher than rates among other students from similar backgrounds
    c.   are lower than rates among other students only for girls and women
    d.   are higher among athletes in golf and tennis than among athletes in football and basketball

29. Data presented in the chapter show that rates of alcohol use and binge drinking are generally higher among student-athletes than among other students. The author suggests that this difference may be related to
    a.   the genetic make-up of people with athletic skills
    b.   weak character among those who play sports
    c.   the fact that athletes are frequently older than other students in their schools
    d.   group dynamics on sport teams that generally encourage overconformity to group norms*

30. Data on sexual assault rates among male athletes are difficult to collect. Some data do suggest that male athletes in certain sports have higher sexual assault rates than other men. The author suggests that this may be related to the
    a.   deprivation of living in athletic dormitories
    b.   drinking behavior of athletes
    c.   dynamics of all-male groups in which there is an emphasis on physical dominance over others*
    d.   psychological strains of being in the public eye so much of the time

31. The results of Michael Trulson's study summarized in the boxed section indicate that involvement in sports may lead to positive changes in the characteristics of juvenile delinquents when playing sports is combined with an emphasis on
    a.   trying to be the best the person can be
    b.   just saying no to deviance
    c.   a philosophy of nonviolence and respect for self and others*
    d.   using psychological techniques to manage stress and confront problems directly

32. At the close of the boxed section entitled, "Is sport participation a 'cure' for deviant behavior?" the author concludes that good outcomes are most likely when
    a.   sport participation puts young people in contact with supportive adults and with the rest of the community*
    b.   young people play on teams that have good coaches and winning records
    c.   strong bonds are formed between athletes on the same teams
    d.   the programs are organized and controlled by authority figures such as police or teachers

33. Evidence presented in the chapter shows that performance-enhancing drugs have been used
    a.   over many centuries by athletes from different countries and in different sports*
    b.   in every Olympic sport since the first modern Olympic Games in 1896
    c.   only since sports has been widely covered by television
    d.   only since the 1950s in Europe and since the 1960s in the U.S.

34. According to the "substance availability hypothesis" described in the chapter, most substance use and abuse is tied to
    a.   an overcommitment to the sport ethic among athletes*
    b.   a lack of dedication among athletes
    c.   defective socialization among athletes
    d.   a lack of moral character among athletes

35. Defining and banning performance enhancing drugs is difficult because
    a.   people in sports actually favor the use of drugs by athletes
    b.   most athletes lack confidence in their physical skills
    c.   most athletes are not concerned with issues of fairness
    d.   it is difficult to define what substances are "natural" and "artificial"*

36. The analysis in the text leads to the conclusion that efforts to control the use of performance-enhancing drugs in sports will only be effective if they involve
    a. appeals to the personal values of athletes themselves
    b. education programs emphasizing the dangers of drug use
    c. appeals for "fair play" within sports
    d. a critical examination of the norms that exist in sports*

37. According to the author, deciding which drugs really do aid performance and which drugs should be banned is often difficult because lab studies on the performance-enhancing properties of drugs are limited in that
    a. medical researchers do not use the same drug dosages in their studies that athletes do in their personal lives*
    b. drug companies have discouraged research on all hormones, including steroids
    c. most athletes are afraid to take steroids as medical subjects
    d. there are no experienced physicians who will supervise studies of steroids

38. Many arguments for banning the use of performance enhancing drugs are based on the belief that such drugs can be harmful to the health of athletes. These arguments are difficult to make to athletes because
    a. their coaches and trainers have sheltered them from knowledge about injuries
    b. many athletes have learned to live with health risks in their sports*
    c. medical researchers can tell us little about health risks and substance use
    d. most drugs have no negative side affects

39. According to the history of drug testing in sports, when tests were developed to detect the use of anabolic steroids, many athletes switched to the use of other substances including the more dangerous substances of
    a. testosterone and human growth hormone*
    b. heroin and cocaine
    c. marijuana and alcohol
    d. "beta-blockers" and "uppers"

40. According to the rules of the IOC, athletes will not test positive for testosterone unless they
    a. have taken anabolic steroids with the testosterone
    b. are found to have six times above normal amounts in their systems*
    c. have taken oil-based rather than water-based dosages
    d. are also taking diuretics with the testosterone

41. Arguments against the use of drug testing in sports often emphasize that testing does not work as a deterrent and that random, mandatory testing
    a. is a violation of a person's right to privacy*
    b. can't be done because there is a shortage of chemists to do the testing
    c. interferes with the trust between athletes and coaches
    d. is itself a health hazard

42. According to the author, a drug-testing program will not be effective unless all athletes are convinced that the testing program is organized so that
    a.   only physically dangerous drugs are banned
    b.   precise testing times are clearly announced to all athletes in the same sport
    c.   penalties for positive tests do not affect an athlete's participation in future events
    d.   all users of all performance-enhancing drugs are identified and punished without any exceptions*

43. The author's policy recommendations for controlling substance use in sports calls for a drug-control policy based on
    a.   critical theory*
    b.   conflict theory
    c.   feminism
    d.   functionalism

44. The author's policy recommendations for controlling substance use in sports call for a drug-control policy that involves
    a.   questioning norms and setting limits on conformity in sports*
    b.   better surveillance and detection procedures
    c.   the need for athletes to conform without question to coaches' rules
    d.   the use of sport science to legally improve performance in sports

45. One of the author's suggestions for controlling the use of performance-enhancing substances is to replace traditional drug education programs with
    a.   blood-testing and DNA-testing programs
    b.   programs on nutritional supplements
    c.   programs on biofeedback and stress management
    d.   deviance and health education programs

ESSAY QUESTIONS

1. One of your classmates in a sociology course on deviant behavior decides to do a paper on deviance in sport. He cannot find any good studies on the topic. He comes to you for an explanation. How do you explain to him that studying deviance in sport presents unique problems and that few people have been able to publish work on the topic?

2. After reading a news article on pro and college athletes who have been arrested lately, your father tells you that deviance is simply out of control in sports today. He also says that if he was in charge of sports, he would control deviance among athletes by strictly enforcing rules based on the ideals of sport, and that he would punish anyone caught breaking the rules. What conceptual approach to deviance is your father using, and how would you explain to him that his approach has serious weaknesses?

3. After reading a news article on highlighting coaches' complaints about what they see as "strange" behavior among athletes today, one of your friends tells you she is tired of seeing some athletes labeled as deviants because their behavior does not meet the expectations of the powerful people who control sports. She argues that deviance in sport would stop being a problem if sports were reorganized so athletes made the rules and the profit motive was eliminated. Describe the conceptual approach your friend is using, and point out the weaknesses in her argument.

4. One of your friends who is always talking about the need for a strict "law and order" approach to crime tells you that athletes who take testosterone, anabolic steroids, or growth hormones in locker rooms are no different than heroin addicts who shoot up in the streets. How would you use the "critical normal distribution approach" to explain that there are differences in the dynamics of these two types of drug use, and that these differences must be recognized if drug use in sports is to be controlled?

5. An officer in your school's ROTC program gives a speech in which he praises soldiers who risk injury, make sacrifices, put their lives on the line, and sometimes die for their countries. Later in the speech, he condemns the use of performance-enhancing drugs in sport and accuses the athletes who use them of lacking character and discipline. As a reporter for your school newspaper, how could you use the material in this chapter to critique the officer's speech in your write-up for the paper?

6. After reading the material on positive deviance, use your own experience (as an athlete or spectator or friend of an athlete) to identify a form of positive deviance in sports. Then explain the origins of the deviance and a course of action a coach might take to control this form of deviance among his/her athletes.

7. A youth football coach tells your son and his fellow teammates that if they want to play football they will have to make sacrifices, learn to play with pain and ignore injuries, and generally "pay the price" to be an athlete. You want your son to conform to the norms of sport, but you realize that overconformity to norms could lead to serious trouble. How might overconformity become a problem, and what would you tell your son about following the coach's advice?

8. As a reporter for your school newspaper, you are asked to do an investigative story about off-the-field deviance among members of the varsity football team. You review the research on the topic and decide to conduct a study on your campus. What did you learn from past research, and how would you use that research as a basis for designing your own study?

9. Rates of binge drinking and sexual assault seem to be higher among male athletes than among other students on college campuses. Male athletes claim they are no different than other all-male groups on campus, including fraternities and the predominantly male ROTC student group. What are the characteristics of these all-male groups that might be related to these forms of deviance? What forms of intervention might be effective in controlling binge drinking and sexual assault on campus?

10. As a new worker in a juvenile treatment center, you have been asked to design a sport-participation program for delinquent adolescents. Your supervisor says all the boys in the program measure high in aggressiveness, and he wants you to organize a "nonaggressive" sport experience for them. You suggest a traditional tae kwon do program, and he asks you why you think a martial art could ever lead to decreases in aggressive tendencies. How would you defend your suggestion?

11. The chapter in the text focuses heavily on issues related to deviance among athletes. But athletes are not the only people in sports who violate norms. Using information from your own experience or from what has occurred recently in sports in your country, community, or on your campus, identify examples of deviant behavior among people in sports other than athletes. Are these forms of deviance new, or have they existed also in the past?

12. Your local newspaper prints an editorial in which the use of performance enhancing drugs in sport is blamed on profit motives, commercial interest, television coverage, and the erosion of traditional values. You decide to write a letter to the editor disagreeing with the editorial. How would your letter read?

13. The definition of what constitutes drug use in sport, and what should be done to control drug use is a controversial topic. "Doping" (i.e., drug use) was first defined by the IOC in 1967, and the first drug tests were administered in 1968. However, it is clear that the use of performance-enhancing drugs has increased since the time of the first tests. Why hasn't testing been a deterrent?

14. You have been appointed the chairperson of a President's Commission on Drug Use in Sport. In setting the agenda for your committee members, you indicate that the major task will be to critically examine the norms and structure of sport. How would you convince the committee members that this is important to your goal of developing policy recommendations for controlling drug use in sport?

15. You are taking a mid-term exam in your sociology of sport course. You must have a good grade to maintain the GPA that you think you should maintain as a serious student. You take an over-the-counter caffeine supplement so you can study all night. You get an A but your instructor discovers your test score was drug-aided. Should your A be turned to an F? Should you be put on academic probation? How is your situation different from the distance runner who was discovered to have used EPO before a race he won at a track meet?

16. Athletes from an Asian country are winning a large share of medals in distance events in running and swimming. It is discovered that their abilities are partially related to a special herb they include in their diet, and the herb only grows in the special high-altitude environment in which the Asian runners train. Should the herb be put on the banned-substance list? What are all the issues that need to be considered when answering this question?

17. After reading Chapter 6 do you think it is possible to have elite sports in which the use of performance enhancing substances does not occur? If you say "yes," then explain how you would maintain a "substance free" environment. If your answer is "no," then explain why it is not possible.

18. The year is 2020. Your 15-year-old daughter comes to you and says she wants to take a new drug that will help make her a track star in high school. The drug is cheap, it has no known side effects, it is not illegal, and other athletes are taking it. You tell your daughter you don't want her taking the drug, and she demands an explanation. How do you justify your position?

CHAPTER 7
AGGRESSION IN SOCIETY:
do sports control or encourage aggressive behavior?

CHAPTER OUTLINE

I.   What is aggression?

II.   Do sports control and moderate aggression in society?
        A.   Human instincts and aggression
                1.   Problems with instinct theory
        B.   Frustration and aggression
        C.   Learning to control aggression by playing sports

III.   Do sports promote aggression in society?
        A.   Sport experiences, frustration, and aggression
        B.   Sport experiences and learning to use aggression as a strategy
                1.   Noncontact sports
                2.   Contact sports: male athletes
                        a.   How is violence connected with ideas about masculinity and race?
                3.   Contact sports: female athletes
        C.   Sports, violence, and the gender order

IV.   Sports and aggression among spectators
        A.   The effects of watching sports on television
                1.   Violence as media entertainment and entertainers as models
        B.   The effects of attending sport events in person
                1.   Violence and action in the event
                2.   Violence, crowd dynamics, and situational factors
                3.   Violence and the overall context in which the event occurs
        C.   Controlling spectator violence

V.   Conclusion: cure or cause?

MULTIPLE CHOICE QUESTIONS

1.   In the chapter introduction, it is noted that research findings as well as popular statements and conclusions about sports and aggression are often full of contradictions. Which of the following is *not* among the reasons the author gives for the existence of contradictory statements and conclusions?
     a.   the short-term effects of playing or watching sports are not distinguished from long term effects
     b.   important terms are not defined precisely
     c.   all sport forms are lumped together regardless of their purpose and organization
     d.   players and spectators are treated differently when the dynamics of aggression are the same for both*

2.   As defined in the chapter, aggression is most closely related to which of the following?
     a.   assertive behavior
     b.   competitive behavior
     c.   destructive or injurious behavior*
     d.   achievement-oriented behavior

3.   As defined in the chapter, violence refers to
     a.   all acts of physical aggression*
     b.   any act that intimidates another person
     c.   behaviors that are irrational
     d.   instinctive behavior directed against another human being

4.   The idea that sport provides a safe outlet for genetically based aggressive behavior is grounded primarily in the ideas of
     a.   learning theorists
     b.   conflict theorists
     c.   self-concept theorists
     d.   Freudian theorists*

5.   Some ethologists (scientists who study behavior patterns among birds, fish, and animals) have argued that
     a.   aggression is primarily learned behavior
     b.   sports create a need for aggression
     c.   aggressive behavior among all animals, including humans, is grounded in instincts*
     d.   aggression ultimately leads to the destruction of any animal species

6. One of the major problems with using instinct theory to argue that sports are a cure for aggressive behavior in society is that
   a. there is no research to support the idea that humans have aggressive instincts or that sport serves as catharsis for these instincts*
   b. aggressive instincts vary widely from one group of people to another
   c. instinct theory can only be used to explain the behavior of people at the early stages of evolutionary development
   d. sport attracts people who have strong instincts

7. According to the research findings of anthropologist Richard Sipes (cited in the chapter), contact sports are most likely to be found in societies that have
   a. democratic governments
   b. long traditions of fighting many wars*
   c. long records of peaceful relationships with other societies
   d. weak prison systems

8. If playing an hour of racquetball after a frustrating day at work makes a person less aggressive, it is probably because the activity
   a. produces physical exhaustion
   b. puts time between the person and the source of frustration*
   c. enables the participant to transfer aggressive feelings into the racquetball itself
   d. changes the source of frustration to the opponent on the court

9. According to the author, sport participation may, under certain conditions, create frustration. This is most likely to occur when people use sports as a means for
   a. self-fulfillment and personal satisfaction
   b. meeting other people or reaffirming personal relationships
   c. developing physical skills and competence
   d. proving something to themselves or others*

10. Research suggests that sport participation may provide people with experiences that help them learn to control aggressive behavior in their own lives. This has occurred in connection with martial arts participation when
    a. the students are committed to competitive success in their martial art
    b. the instructor teaches students how to use their bodies as weapons
    c. the students all come from middle-class backgrounds
    d. the instructor emphasizes a philosophy of nonviolence and focuses on the mastery of skills*

11. Quotes from the boxers interviewed by Loic Wacquant, in his study of the culture and experiences associated with a boxing gym in a ghetto area in Chicago, indicate that the boxers
   a. were eager to use their skills on the streets to protect themselves
   b. learned their craft in ways that encouraged them to control the expression of aggressive behaviors*
   c. joined the gym to learn violence in an organized setting
   d. were motivated primarily by a hate for fellow boxers, especially those from other gyms

12. The author argues that we should not expect sport participation to teach people how to control aggression because
   a. most athletes have strong instincts to be aggressive
   b. coaches have personalities that measure very high on aggressive tendencies
   c. dominant sport forms often emphasize hostility and physical domination of others*
   d. success in sports requires a lack of self-control in any form

13. According to the model presented by the author, frustration is most likely to lead to aggressive behavior when it is accompanied by an emotional response of
   a. depression
   b. active anxiety
   c. anger*
   d. embarrassment

14. Research reviewed in the chapter shows that aggressive behavior is most likely to be a result of frustration when the situation contains
   a. people with poor social skills
   b. opportunities and stimulus cues for violence*
   c. emotional facilitators and high density
   d. many uniformed security guards

15. The author notes that in the case of spectators, the relationship between frustration and aggressive behavior partially depends on the extent to which spectators
   a. are committed to the spectator role
   b. have been associated with one another in the past
   c. see sport as a form of emotional expression
   d. identify with the players or the teams involved*

16. In the discussion of whether athletes learn to use aggression as a strategy in sports, the author notes that rule-violating behaviors in sports are most likely to be accepted by athletes in
   a. noncontact sports
   b. heavy contact sports*
   c. sports which attract spectators from upper-income groups
   d. sports in which there is no protective equipment used by players

17. In the discussion of whether athletes learn to use aggression as a strategy in noncontact sports, the author argues that players in noncontact sports
    a. are seldom rewarded for aggressive behaviors*
    b. are taught to use intimidation and aggression in psychological as well as physical terms
    c. are the most aggressive of any athletes when it comes to psychological intimidation
    d. have more opportunities to use intimidation than athletes in contact sports

18. Research reviewed by the author suggests that as the amount of contact increases in a sport, athletes
    a. increasingly accept violence as a part of sport participation*
    b. develop norms that discourage the use of intimidation or violence
    c. purposely use violence to disrupt the flow of action in games
    d. become more motivated to inflict career ending injuries on opponents

19. The author argues that in the culture of heavy contact sports, there is a general norm emphasizing the following message:
    a. violence creates more harmful violence
    b. fighting loses games but wins fans
    c. aggressive players have short careers
    d. be aggressive or get out*

20. According to the author's explanation, the person who plays the role of "enforcer" on a contact sport team is expected to
    a. assist referees in controlling the game
    b. intimidate opponents*
    c. provide legal advice to teammates
    d. aggravate the coach of the opposing team

21. According to the material presented in the chapter, which of the following statements about aggression in contact sports is *not* true?
    a. boys and men in contact sports learn that they will be evaluated on their ability to use violence
    b. athletes who identify with violent professional players are more violent in their own games
    c. the behavior of enforcers is caused by a combination of frustration and anger*
    d. being recognized by teammates as an athlete requires being able to give and take aggression

22. The author suggests that the media coverage of contact sports, and the videos that portray action in these sports, are full of references and examples that
    a. discourage the use of violence on the field
    b. present violence as a normal and exciting part of the game*
    c. suggest that violent players be banned from sports
    d. prove that violence destroys drama in sports

23. Do athletes who learn to use violent strategies on the playing field also use these strategies off the field? The research on this question leads the author to conclude that carryover
    a. definitely occurs, and it is very dangerous
    b. never occurs because athletes know the difference between sports and the rest of their lives
    c. only occurs in the case of older athletes who have had poor relationships with their fathers
    d. has not, at this point, been proven to occur in a regular or identifiable pattern*

24. According to the author, the use of aggressive behavior in sports has come to be defined as "normal" by many people because being able to "do" violence is seen as
    a. a means for males to prove their "manhood"*
    b. necessary if a person is to be a good leader
    c. a way to protect one's health and well-being
    d. an important part of being human

25. Research done by Michael Messner (reviewed in the chapter) suggests that most athletes see injurious acts as forms of violence only when they are
    a. done with intent to hurt
    b. not identified by referees
    c. not done within the rules of the game*
    d. motivated by true anger

26. The author argues that men can be encouraged to do extremely violent things on the playing field when they
    a. have reputations as "nice people" off the field
    b. are desperate to avoid labels like "pussy" or "fag" that challenge their masculinity*
    c. define masculinity in terms of being able to avoid violence
    d. have close personal relationships with family members, especially their fathers

27. According to the author, gender and race get connected with aggression in sports when people have stereotypes that lead them to see
    a. white men as dangerous
    b. black women as vulnerable
    c. white men and black men as natural enemies
    d. black men as intimidating*

28. The author argues that if we want to understand more about the relationship between sports and violence, we must learn more about
   a. connections between the social worlds created around sports and other aspects of community life*
   b. the personalities of athletes and those who coach them
   c. the dynamic connection between frustration and human instincts
   d. the social and family backgrounds of those who are selected to play elite sports

29. The author argues that if we want to understand more about the relationship between sports and violence, we must learn more about issues that go beyond sports. Which of the following is *not* related to the issues identified by the author?
   a. identity and hubris
   b. masculinity and misogyny
   c. racism and stereotypes
   d. attitudes and cognitive dissonance*

30. Research on female athletes in contact sports suggests that women are
   a. genetically predisposed to be less violent than men are
   b. more likely than men to be violent in response to the commands of a coach
   c. less likely than men to use their ability to do violence as proof of their sexual identity*
   d. becoming less and less violent in sports as the stakes for success in sports become greater

31. According to the author, some men glorify and celebrate the violence done by male athletes because examples of male aggression can be used to preserve
   a. the purity of sports
   b. traditional ideas about sex and gender differences*
   c. the idea that men are smarter than women
   d. the overall health and physical well being of men

32. The author argues that women should be careful not to buy into the same aggressive orientations used by some men in sports because these orientations
   a. are immoral according to most religious belief systems
   b. are disapproved of by the majority of people in society
   c. are necessary for men to feel good about themselves and their place in society
   d. reaffirm a power and performance approach to sports that in the long run privileges men over women*

33. The author argues that it is very difficult to eliminate violence in certain sports because when athletes face and use violence and endure its consequences in their lives, they experience a form of drama that creates
    a. fantasies about what the world is like apart from sports
    b. a strong desire to retire from sport and enjoy life
    c. strong emotional bonds that tie athletes together in special and memorable ways*
    d. fears about health and well being

34. According to the author, watching sports on television often leads viewers to be
    a. so hostile that it creates a context in which aggression is common
    b. emotionally expressive, but it seldom incites aggressive behavior*
    c. targets of aggressive acts on the part of those not watching sports
    d. frustrated, angry, and aggressive, especially when they are watching with a crowd

35. Research shows that watching violence in sports
    a. automatically leads to immediate patterns of imitation in sport behavior
    b. has serious short-term effects but no long-term effects
    c. makes people less sensitive to the feelings of others
    d. does not seem to have short-term effects on how most adults play sports*

36. The author hypothesizes that violence in sports
    a. causes people to approve of all violence in a moral sense
    b. is most entertaining when it regularly disrupts the action in a game
    c. attracts female fans more than it does male fans because it is more shocking to females
    d. is least entertaining when it interferes with goal achievement during a game*

37. While discussing violence among spectators who attend events in person, the author points out that sport fans are
    a. more disorderly than people at other mass events
    b. generally well-behaved and aware of norms for behavior*
    c. unaware of norms for behavior while events are in progress
    d. likely to encourage one another to be destructive

38. Research suggests that spectators are most likely to engage in violence themselves when they interpret the actions of players to be
    a. violent*
    b. emotionally intense
    c. uncontrolled
    d. product-oriented

39. In the discussion of violence, crowd dynamics, and situational factors, the author concludes that
    a.   because of location factors, spectator violence would be more likely at a Manchester United vs Liverpool soccer game than at a San Francisco 49ers vs Miami Dolphins football game*
    b.   soccer violence is a problem because British people are generally more violent than North Americans
    c.   spectator violence could be eliminated if sport facilities used control systems like those used in prison camps
    d.   situational factors are not as important as the personality profiles of regular spectators at an event

40. Information on spectator violence throughout history suggests that the worst cases of violence have usually been related to
    a.   the amount of media coverage given to a game or match
    b.   issues and tensions that were important in the community as a whole*
    c.   efforts to control the amount of alcohol available at the game or match
    d.   the number of uniformed police in the stadium or arena

41. In Rollo May's analysis of the causes of violence in society, he concludes that violence
    a.   is caused by having too much power and too many resources
    b.   among humans is caused by the same factors that cause other animals to be violent
    c.   may be used by powerless people to achieve feelings of personal significance*
    d.   is usually related to sexual issues and relationships

42. Which of the following is *not* among the author's policy recommendations for controlling sport violence
    a.   respecting the needs and rights of the spectators
    b.   limiting violence among athletes playing in events
    c.   establishing relationships between communities and teams and facilities
    d.   banning all block sales of tickets to large groups of people*

ESSAY QUESTIONS

1. "Aggression" is a widely used term in connection with sports. Why is it necessary to develop a precise definition of aggression and related terms when studying sports?

2. You are in a class where the students are debating whether boxing should be banned in your country. One side says boxing glorifies and therefore promotes aggressive behavior in the rest of society; the other side says boxing serves as an outlet for aggressive energy and therefore controls aggression. Which position do you feel is most defensible? Explain the strengths of the position you side with and explain the weaknesses of the other position.

3. It is popularly believed that aggressive behavior is grounded in instincts and that sports provide harmless outlets for instinctive aggressive behaviors. What are the major problems with using instinct theory to discuss the relationship between sport and violence?

4. It is widely believed that sport participation relieves the frustration created by everyday life experiences and therefore decreases the likelihood for aggressive behavior. What are the circumstances under which sport participation is most likely to make people less frustrated and therefore less apt to be aggressive?

5. There are numerous cases where athletes have to control aggressive behavior on the playing field. Some people say that this means athletes are learning to control the same tendencies off the field. What are the major problems with this conclusion?

6. Most sports generate a certain amount of frustration among participants. However, frustration does not always lead to aggressive behavior. What conditions must be present before aggression among athletes is likely to be a response to frustration?

7. Using what is now known about the relationship between frustration and aggression, describe a situation in which spectators would be most likely to engage in aggressive behavior at a sport event. In other words, what are the conditions that would be necessary for spectators to experience frustration and then have this frustration converted into aggressive behavior?

8. You work in a juvenile treatment center. Your boss says she wants you to develop a boxing program for the boys in the program so they will have a chance to "work out their aggressive feelings and become well-adjusted human beings in the process." She then gives you an opportunity to respond to her idea. What would you say?

9. Violence among young people is defined as a problem in your city. Some people argue that there is a need to fund more sport programs so young people can have an outlet for their aggressive impulses and energy. As a school board member, would you vote to increase funding for more sport programs on the basis of this argument? Use material in Chapter 7 to support your position.

10. The use of intimidation as a strategy has become common in certain sports. Explain why this has occurred and provide examples to show how intimidation is used as a strategy by athletes and teams. Why has this happened and what can be done to reverse the trend?

11. Aggression in sports does not occur in a social vacuum. Rates of aggression among athletes may be related to gender and race relations in society. Explain how gender and race relations may be related to displays of aggression in sports?

12. You and your uncle are watching a game in the ABL. During the game one of the players elbows her opponent in the face. Your uncle says that it won't be long until the level of violence in women's sports matches the violence in men's sports. He further explains that women can be more violent than men. How would you respond to your uncle? Explain why you would agree or disagree with him.

13. Violence among spectators can be a serious problem. Some people say that this problem exists because people learn violent behavior patterns while they are watching sports. Evaluate this hypothesis on the basis of materials in the book. Also explain whether you a more violent person because you have watched sports on television.

14. After reading a news account of a case of "soccer hooliganism" in England, your friend says that North Americans must be more civilized than the English because "hooliganism" does not seem to be a problem in the U.S. or Canada. How would you inform your friend that the English are no less civilized than North Americans, and that there are major differences in situational factors that influence spectator violence in these two settings?

15. You are hosting an in-state rivalry game between your #1-ranked football team and the #2-ranked team in your division. Violence has occurred at this game in previous years. After reading the chapter, what measures would you take to control player and spectator violence on and off the field?

CHAPTER 8
GENDER:
is equity the only issue?

CHAPTER OUTLINE

I.   Participation and equity issues
    A.   Participation patterns among women
        1.   Why participation has increased
            a.   New opportunities
            b.   Government legislation
            c.   The women's movement
            d.   The health and fitness movement
            e.   Increased media coverage of women's sports
        2.   Reasons to be cautious when predicting future participation increases
            a.   Budget cutbacks and the privatization of sport programs
            b.   Resistance to government policies and legislation
            c.   Backlash among those who resent changes favoring strong women
            d.   Underrepresentation of women in coaching and power positions in sports
            e.   Continued emphasis on "cosmetic fitness"
            f.   The trivialization of certain women athletes and women's sports
    (BOX: "Cheerleaders: the 'side-show' of American sports?")
    B.   Gender inequities in sports
        1.   Participation opportunities
        2.   Support for athletes
        3.   Jobs for women in coaching and administration
    C.   What changes are needed to achieve gender equity?
        1.   Sport participation, personal empowerment, and striving for equity
        2.   Men's interest in gender equity

II.   Ideological and structural issues
    A.   The "gender logic" of sports
    B.   From "gender logic" to ideology: sports as a celebration of masculinity
    C.   Ideology in action: the social construction of "sissies" and "tomboys"
    D.   Need for ideological and structural changes
        1.   Alternative definitions of masculinity
        2.   Alternative definitions of femininity
    (BOX: "Women bodybuilders: expanding definitions of femininity?")
        3.   Changing the way we "do" sports

III.   Conclusion: is equity the only issue?

MULTIPLE CHOICE QUESTIONS

1.   The author claims that the single most dramatic change in the world of sport since the early 1970s has been
      a.   the number of lawsuits filed by men who have resisted attempts to provide opportunities for girls and women
      b.   the number of women who have become coaches and administrators in men's sport programs
      c.   the number of mothers who are now coaching their daughters in youth sport programs
      d.   increased sport participation among girls and women around the world*

2.   Since the early 1970s there have been a number of reasons for increased sport participation rates among girls and women. Which of the following is *not* among the reasons given by the author to explain the increases?
      a.   new publicly funded child care programs*
      b.   new opportunities for sport participation
      c.   the women's movement
      d.   the health and fitness movement

3.   Title IX of the Education Amendments has been U.S. law since 1972. According to this law, it is
      a.   illegal to keep women out of any school sport programs funded by the regular budget
      b.   recommended that males and females be provided exactly the same sports in school programs
      c.   illegal to deny any person on the basis of sex the benefits of an educational program receiving federal assistance*
      d.   mandated that boys and girls be allowed to try out for the same teams

4.   The author notes that on a global basis women have been effective in getting people around the world to acknowledge the importance of sport and physical education opportunities for girls and women by
      a.   arguing that these opportunities promote the education, health, and human rights of girls and women*
      b.   socializing their own daughters to be physically active
      c.   applying pressure on religious organizations to change their teachings about women
      d.   directly supporting the goals of men in established sport organizations around the world

5. In the discussion about the consequences of increased media coverage of women in sports, the author concludes that seeing women athletes on television
    a. shows girls that sports are male activities in which they can participate when men encourage them
    b. leads men to be less supportive of increased sport opportunities for girls and women
    c. turns many girls off to sport participation because they don't like how the athletes look
    d. is especially important for girls because they often get mixed messages about becoming serious athletes*

6. The author suggests that there are a number of reasons to be cautious about predicting a further expansion of sport participation among women. Which of the following was *not* among those reasons?
    a. budgets for women's athletics are often vulnerable to cuts and they seldom allow for covering high start up costs
    b. some people generally resist government legislation calling for gender equity
    c. women are less likely to enjoy themselves than men do when they participate in sports*
    d. there is a relative lack of women in coaching and power positions in sports

7. The author argues that as sport programs become increasingly privatized, the future participation increases among women will be
    a. highest among those who receive public assistance from the government
    b. unevenly distributed, with those lacking resources suffering setbacks*
    c. reversed in all segments of the population
    d. highest in programs where men and women play sports together

8. According to the author, an emphasis on "cosmetic fitness" and thinness among women can have a negative effect on sport participation because it leads women to
    a. eat too much protein and not enough carbohydrates to maintain energy levels
    b. wear clothes that are bulky and restrict movement
    c. play only those sports that involve strength and speed
    d. associate sport participation with losing weight and becoming sexually attractive*

9. According to the examples provided by the author, women's sports can be trivialized through
    a. the use of team nicknames and mascots inconsistent with physical competence*
    b. publicizing injury rates among women athletes
    c. allowing too many women's teams to be coached by women
    d. trying too hard to eliminate homophobia in sports

10. Historical accounts indicate that before the 1940s, cheerleading was
    a. defined as a "ladylike" activity
    b. organized to systematically exclude men
    c. an activity that some people thought would masculinize women*
    d. seen as being naturally suited for women

11. In the discussion of cheerleading today, the author argues that
    a. male athletes frequently define cheerleaders as crucial to team success
    b. being a cheerleader is no longer an important source of status and popularity in U.S. high schools
    c. the role of cheerleader generally maintains traditional definitions of femininity*
    d. cheerleaders have lower levels of self-esteem than their peers

12. The author claims that girls and women who play sports encounter the strongest resistance to their sport participation when they
    a. are successful at winning medals in international competitions
    b. play sports that have traditionally been used as symbols of masculinity in the culture*
    c. emphasize grace and beauty in their competitions
    d. participate in large groups under the supervision of women coaches and administrators

13. Information on gender equity and the modern Summer Olympic Games illustrates that
    a. fewer Olympic events are open to women than to men and male athletes outnumber female athletes by nearly 2:1*
    b. women have more events, but fewer participants in those events than the men have
    c. the proportion of women athletes in the games has steadily declined since the turn of the century
    d. since the 1980 Moscow Olympics, about half of the athletes in the summer games have been women

14. The author points out that when it comes to the issue of equal support for athletes,
    a. nearly all sport-sponsoring organizations have achieved true gender equity
    b. women now receive 50% of all the resources, but they don't receive 50% of the publicity and media coverage
    c. enforcement of the law has been difficult because opposition has been strong*
    d. women have been most successful when they do not pressure men to make changes

15.	The author reviews data on jobs for women in coaching and administration in U.S. intercollegiate sports. Which of the following *contradicts* the main findings reported in the chapter?
	a.	between 1977 and 1996, the proportion of women coaching women's teams has decreased in nine of the top 10 women's intercollegiate sports
	b.	less than 15% of the most influential people in college sports are women
	c.	when women's sport programs have women athletic directors, there is a higher proportion of women in coaching positions
	d.	women have lost jobs at all levels, but especially in the lowest-paying jobs where opportunities are most plentiful*

16.	The author notes that if men encountered the same patterns encountered by women in coaching and administration in most sport organizations, the men would
	a.	reject the need for affirmative action to improve their situation
	b.	be outraged by the lack of equity*
	c.	be satisfied with their progress
	d.	praise women for their support of men's programs and opportunities

17.	There are a number of reasons for the underrepresentation of women in coaching and administrative positions. According to the author, which of the following is *not* one of those reasons?
	a.	men are more likely to be perceived as qualified for these positions than are women
	b.	men are more apt to be in positions to determine who gets jobs in women's programs
	c.	women often do not have the time or the experience to make policy in athletic programs*
	d.	women don't yet have networks and connections in the sport world that are as effective as those men have

18.	The author claims that most men support the idea of gender equity, but few of them are willing to sacrifice men's past privilege to actually achieve equity. This, according to the author, has forced those interested in equity to
	a.	ask governments for assistance and take legal action when possible*
	b.	join organizations that oppose all forms of organized sports
	c.	to abandon their idealism and simply support existing men's sports
	d.	reject government assistance in favor of seeking corporate support

19.	Donna Lopiano, director of the Women's Sport Foundation, urges people to use certain strategies to promote gender equity. As discussed in the chapter, her strategies emphasize
	a.	working "behind the scenes" so as to avoid confrontation
	b.	supporting the men in power positions so they will treat women fairly
	c.	getting organized and persistently struggling against inequities*
	d.	forgetting about keeping track of numbers and focusing on general principles

20.   According to the author, many people in the sociology of sport have argued that real gender equity will never be achieved in sports as long as
a.   women do not play football and other heavy contact sports
b.   sports activities are shaped primarily by the values and experiences of men*
c.   females are not able to match males in strength and speed
d.   advocates of equity encourage the development of new models of sport participation

21.   After reviewing data on the impact of sport participation on girls and women, the author notes that women feel certain things when they develop strength through sport participation. Which of the following is *not* one of the things women feel?
a.   that they are physically competent
b.   that they are more in control of their physical safety
c.   that their bodies are objects to be assessed by others*
d.   that they are less vulnerable

22.   Data collected from women in sports suggests that playing traditional sports contributes to feelings of empowerment on the personal level,
a.   but it does not make women more aware of and active in connection with gender issues in society as a whole*
b.   and turns most younger women into outspoken feminists
c.   but these feelings are rejected as soon as sport participation ceases
d.   and leads them to reject sports in which aggression and competition are highlighted

23.   The author notes that men also have an interest in gender equity. This is because efforts to achieve gender equity
a.   will provide men with advantages when they seek jobs in new women's sport programs
b.   make women more helpful partners and co-workers
c.   make men more aware of the need to be assertive while competing against others
d.   will involve new sport participation opportunities not based on dominant definitions of masculinity*

24.   The author points out that a gender equity panel of the NCAA has said that a useful method of determining if gender equity exists in sport programs is to see if
a.   men are happy with the way resources are allocated to both women and men
b.   people in the men's and women's programs would trade places with their counterparts in the program of the other gender*
c.   athletes in both the men's and women's programs enjoy playing their sports
d.   the coaches in all sports have the same turnover rates

25. The author argues that achieving a total form of gender equity in sports requires
    a. a clear measurement of the allocation of the material resources used to fund and support sports
    b. a commitment among men to be fair in the way sports are organized
    c. changes in how we think about gender and how we play sports*
    d. the elimination of all men from women's programs

26. According to the author, the "gender logic" that has been used widely by people in sports generally emphasized that
    a. men and women were physically different but equal
    b. women were naturally superior to men when it came to performance in certain sports
    c. being a women meant being something less than what it meant to be a man in sports*
    d. women have natural aggressive tendencies that make their sports more dangerous than most men's sports

27. According to the material in the chapter, the phrase "she throws like a girl" is grounded in the fact that females
    a. have different shoulder structures than men have
    b. have shorter arms than men
    c. are often seen as physically different from men when it comes to abilities in sports*
    d. participate in sports emphasizing different throwing techniques

28. The author quotes journalist Joan Ryan who has made the case that people in North America and in many other countries like women's figure skating and gymnastics because the athletes in these sports are presented to us in ways that
    a. enable them to avoid the troublesome issues of power, sexual orientation, and aggression that are raised by other female athletes*
    b. highlight the ways in which women athletes have been able to move beyond issues of appearance and beauty
    c. illustrate what it means to be an adult woman in a physical sense
    d. convincingly prove that women can be strong and independent without the support and sponsorship of men

29. The author notes that it is often difficult for us to critically examine cultural ideology because
    a. most people simply take it for granted*
    b. nobody has ever really defined what ideology is
    c. ideology exists only in traditional cultures
    d. ideology is irrelevant in the lives of most people

30. According to the author, dominant gender ideology in many cultures has led to dominant sport forms that
    a. favor the interests of women over men
    b. emphasize character development in the pursuit of excellence
    c. celebrate masculine virility and power*
    d. challenge the idea that men have to be strong and aggressive to be manly

31. The author claims that the images associated with dominant sports in most societies today tend to promote a manhood based on
    a. avoiding all relationships with women
    b. cohesion and intimacy
    c. brotherhood and teamwork
    d. aggression and the ability to dominate others*

32. When athletes on men's teams make mistakes or are seen as not being aggressive enough, their coaches may refer to them as "ladies," "girls," or "fags." According to the author's analysis, these coaches are exhibiting
    a. either misogyny or homophobia or both*
    b. a totally ineffective motivational technique
    c. a form of deviance that most male athletes will report to the coaches' superiors
    d. attitudes that will make his athletes more socially aware of gender issues

33. Gay male athletes respond to homophobia in a number of ways. Which of the following is *not* one of the responses discussed in the chapter (according to Pronger's research)?
    a. some laugh inside at the irony of their participation in an activity that glorifies heterosexuality
    b. some use sports to prove their masculinity to themselves or others
    c. some organize events especially for gay athletes
    d. some confide in and seek support from heterosexual coaches and athletes*

34. Unlike boys who are labeled as "sissies," girls labeled as "tomboys" often receive praise for their behavior. According to the author, this praise
    a. usually continues throughout adolescence and young adulthood
    b. is often combined with negative messages when girls' bodies become sexualized in terms of dominant gender ideology*
    c. is usually reserved for girls and young women who are top-level athletes
    d. comes primarily from women but not from men

35. The author notes that when women athletes have engaged in sports that involve behaviors and orientations that do not fit with dominant definitions of femininity, they can lower their chances of being socially marginalized if they
    a. present themselves in ways that emphasize symbols of heterosexuality*
    b. avoid social situations where nonathletes are present
    c. do not talk about their relationships with boyfriends or husbands
    d. do not dress in typically feminine ways

36. According to research done by Anne Bolin (see the boxed section), women bodybuilders have been frustrated trying to deal with femininity issues in their competitions because
    a.   definitions of femininity tend to shift and change over time*
    b.   they do not see themselves as women in many respects
    c.   judges have a set definition of femininity that they refuse to change
    d.   many people in bodybuilding gyms object to women who want to work out in the same way men do

37. According to the author (see the boxed section), women in power sports have two choices if they want to avoid being socially rejected by many people. Those choices are either to change dominant definitions of femininity or to
    a.   make sure they are ranked champions in their sports
    b.   adopt a lesbian identity regardless of their own sexual orientations
    c.   create an image that fits dominant definitions of femininity*
    d.   avoid competitions that receive media coverage

38. On the basis of what the author says about women bodybuilders and Dennis Rodman, it would be most appropriate to describe Rodman and the bodybuilders as
    a.   people who need serious psychiatric help
    b.   people who push the boundaries of traditional definitions of gender*
    c.   deviants who must be controlled before they erode the moral fibre of society
    d.   introverts who use their bodies to speak to the public

39. According to the author, women bodybuilders often go along with sexualized images of who they are and what they do because
    a.   they realize that muscles are not natural for women
    b.   their workouts are really designed to make them look feminine rather than to build muscles
    c.   it enables them to obtain publicity and endorsement contracts*
    d.   the men in their lives want them to be defined by other men as sexually attractive

40. According to the author, dominant definitions of masculinity are reproduced in connection with many sports. These definitions often encourage men
    a.   to form intimate relationships with other men
    b.   to support and protect the physical well being of girls and women in society
    c.   to engage in behaviors that sometimes jeopardize their own health and well-being*
    d.   to raise questions about violence and destructive behavior

86

41. The author notes that girls in some North American families may be treated differently than their brothers when it comes to sports and physical activities. Which of the following is *not* one of those forms of differential treatment, as discussed in the chapter?
    a. fathers spend less time playing sports with girls
    b. parents are less likely to regulate and control the behavior of their girls*
    c. girls are less likely to learn that sports can be uniquely important sources of rewards in their lives
    d. girls are more likely to receive "conditional permissions" to play sports

42. Young girls in North America are less likely than their brothers to be involved in informal competitive games because
    a. their parents generally discourage them from participating in any physical activities
    b. their parents often give them "conditional permission" to participate in sport activities*
    c. girls have a more difficult time making good friends than boys do
    d. girls learn that they should regularly help their parents around the house

43. According to the author, sports have been sites for the reproduction of traditional ideas about gender while at the same time they have been sites for
    a. showing people that there are no differences between men and women
    b. converting women and men into feminists
    c. showing people that homosexual men can be accepted by teammates and the general public
    d. encouraging people to think in new ways about gender and gender relations*

44. According to the material in the chapter, real gender equity depends on developing alternative definitions of masculinity and femininity along with
    a. changing the way many sports are organized and played*
    b. altering reward systems in sports so men and women can compete against each other
    c. having more women work in men's sports such as football and hockey
    d. drafting new laws calling for equity

45. Creating new sport programs for girls and women is one of the recommended strategies for achieving gender equity. According to the text, the advantage to this strategy is that new programs can
    a. provide new settings for women to learn to be tough competitors
    b. be organized to reflect the values and experiences of women*
    c. exclude men from all positions of responsibility
    d. give women opportunities to learn to dominate other women

46. Creating new sport programs for women can present political problems when it comes to gender issues. Which of the following is *not* one of the problems identified in the chapter?
    a. new sport programs make it difficult to detect and eliminate unequal opportunities
    b. new sport programs run the risk of being perceived as "second class"
    c. new sport programs are more difficult to promote
    d. new sport programs would decrease the number of success-oriented role models available to female athletes*

47. According to the author, ideological and structural changes in sports can be encouraged by new rules emphasizing safety, new rituals bringing opponents together, and
    a. new ways to control athletes who don't conform to expectations
    b. new ways of talking about sports and sport participants*
    c. new opportunities to compete against people from other cultures
    d. new strategies for making women more like men

ESSAY QUESTIONS

1. The chapter lists five reasons why there have been significant increases in the sport participation rates of women in the U.S. Choose the reason you think has been most influential and the reason that has been least influential, and explain why you made your choices.

2. One of your friends reads the first few pages of this chapter and tells you that women have nothing to worry about, that participation increases will continue to occur in the future. You agree that things do look much better than they did 25 years ago, but that there is still reason to be cautious about predicting continued increases in the future. How would you convince your friend that you are correct?

3. The practice of using "Lady" along with other gendered prefixes, suffixes, and nicknames has been a longstanding tradition at many U.S. colleges and universities. What was the original purpose for using these gendered references, and what are the reasons for maintaining these references today? Do you think they should be eliminated? Why or why not?

4. Representatives from the Women's Sport Foundation and the National Association for Girls and Women in Sports have recently noted that although there has been significant progress in connection with equity issues, there is still a long way to go. Do you feel this is an accurate assessment of the past and present? Give examples supporting your agreement or disagreement with this assessment.

5.	A woman has just been hired as the new coach of the women's basketball team at your college/university. A young man in your dorm says that the male applicants for the job never had a chance because the athletic director and the search committee wanted to hire a woman. His inference is that men are not being treated fairly today in the coaching job market. In light of the material in the chapter, and your personal experiences, how would you respond to this young man? Would you agree or disagree with him? Explain your position, and provide data to support your agreement or disagreement.

6.	You have just been appointed as a chairperson of a special committee charged with studying gender equity in your university's sport programs. You must develop a research design and present it to the rest of the committee members. Outline the kinds of data you will collect to assess whether equity has been achieved. What do you expect to find at your university?

7.	You have just been appointed as a chairperson of a special committee charged with promoting gender equity in your university's sport programs. You must develop a strategy for bringing about changes in the future. Outline the strategy proposals you think would be useful. Which of Lopiano's strategies, as listed in the chapter, would you use, and would you add any to her list?

8.	Some feminists who study sports have suggested that woman athletes learn to view their own bodies in positive ways because sport participation enables them to see their bodies as powerful and competent rather than as objects. In other words, women athletes have experiences enabling them to define femininity in ways that contradict traditional definitions of femininity used in the culture. Does this describe your experience or the experience of women you know? If so, give examples; if not, explain why your experiences or the experiences of your friends do not fit with notion of sport participation as a source of empowerment.

9.	You are talking to a man about gender equity. He states that gender equity is strictly a women's issue, and it has nothing to do with him. You are trying to get him to serve on a committee charged with promoting gender equity in your university and the surrounding community. What would you say to him to get him to reconsider his position and agree to serve on your committee?

10.	In the chapter, it is argued that "participation and equity issues" are related to but different from "ideological and structural issues." What are the main differences between these two sets of issues?

11.	Dominant sport forms in most societies tend to reproduce dominant ideas about gender and gender relations. Therefore, when people want to defend the power and privilege that comes with being a man in society, they look to sports, especially heavy contact sports, to support the notion that men and women are different and that men are in ways superior to women. Use the material in the chapter to discuss the notion that sports celebrate traditional ideas about gender and gender relations. Do you agree or disagree with this? Explain your position.

12.   One the one hand, sports can provide women with participation opportunities that are personally empowering; on the other hand, dominant sports tend to perpetuate a gender logic that works to the disadvantage of women in society. How can sports do both these things simultaneously? Which of these outcomes do you think is most important and socially significant in the culture in which you live?

13.   The author claims that the "gender logic" used in dominant sports in the U.S. (Canada, or other countries) turns sports into a celebration of traditional heterosexual masculinity. Have you ever seen gender logic, as defined by the author, used in sports? If you have, provide some examples; if you have not, explain why your experiences differ from what the author describes.

14.   The author makes the case that cheerleaders in U.S. sports generally reaffirm traditional definitions of femininity in ways that ultimately interfere with achieving gender equity in sports. Does your own experience in high school, college, or as a spectator for professional sports fit with the author's argument, or does it contradict it? Explain and give examples to support your response to the author's argument.

15.   Imagine that you are a new teacher in a large high school with a big interscholastic sport program. Your principal has just given you the job of supervising the cheerleaders. How would you handle the job so that you could avoid some of the criticisms of cheerleaders made in the chapter?

16.   According to recent research done by an anthropologist, women bodybuilders often use "femininity insignias" to neutralize the stigma associated with being muscular. What are examples of femininity insignias, and are they ever used by women athletes in sports other than bodybuilding? Provide examples.

17.   Many people describe women bodybuilders in negative terms; some people even refer to them as freaks of nature. Why do some people get so upset at the sight of a muscular woman's body? Are their reactions connected in any way to the gender ideology that exists in this culture? Explain.

18.   There is much disagreement about the extent to which homophobia exists in today's sports (women's and men's). Have you ever heard homophobic fears expressed in connection with any of your experiences in sports (as an athlete or spectator)? If so, explain how they were expressed; if not, explain why homophobia has been absent in any of your experiences.

19.   Your brother has a three-year-old daughter. He tells you that he wants her to be active in sports as she grows up. He also refers to his daughter as "daddy's little girls and mommy's little helper." And he says that daughters are different than sons because they require more protection. What kinds of predictions would you make for your niece's future in sport? Explain the reasons for your predictions.

20. The author claims that real gender equity depends on ideological and structural changes, especially in the way we "do" sports in society. What is meant by this claim? What kinds of ideological and structural changes are needed to bring about gender equity?

CHAPTER 9
RACE AND ETHNICITY:
are skin color and cultural heritage important in sports?

CHAPTER OUTLINE

I.   Culture, sports, and the meaning of race
    A.   Definition of terms
    B.   Origins and implications of the concept of race
    C.   Connecting ideas about race with sports
    (BOX: "Preserving racial ideology through sports")

II.   Racial ideology and sports: a critical analysis
    A.   Using myths to maintain racial ideology
    B.   Race logic in sports: recent examples
    C.   Race logic, gender, and social class
    D.   Race logic and stacking patterns in team sports
    E.   Race logic and jobs in coaching and administration

III.   Sport participation patterns: group by group
    A.   Blacks and sport participation
    B.   Native Americans and sport participation
    (BOX: "Team names, logos, and mascots: when are they indications of bigotry?")
    C.   Hispanics and sport participation
    D.   Asian Americans and sport participation

IV.   The racial desegregation of certain American sports
    A.   The organization of certain sports
    B.   Money and winning: incentives for desegregation
    C.   Perceived opportunities and the development of sport skills
    D.   Why haven't all sports been desegregated?

V.   Sports and intergroup relations
    A.   Racial and ethnic ideologies resist change
    B.   Types of social contacts in sports
    C.   Competition often subverts intergroup cooperation
    D.   Is change possible?
         1.   Noteworthy efforts

VI.   Conclusion: are skin color and cultural heritage important?

MULTIPLE CHOICE QUESTIONS

1. In the author's introduction to the chapter, it is noted that sports are parts of culture that serve as "sites" where
    a. people from all backgrounds are automatically treated as complete equals
    b. being white is irrelevant when it comes to sport participation and sport participation decisions
    c. there are no particular meanings associated with skin color or ethnicity
    d. ideas about skin color and ethnicity are formulated and put into action*

2. Race and ethnicity are two of the terms defined in the chapter. According to those definitions,
    a. race refers to attributes like height while ethnicity refers to skin color
    b. race refers to genetically transmitted traits and ethnicity refers to cultural heritage*
    c. race refers to language and skin color while ethnicity refers to behavior and eating habits
    d. race refers only to minority groups while ethnicity refers to any cultural group in a society

3. Groups socially identified in terms of biological or cultural traits are referred to as "minority groups" if they
    a. come from another country and experience difficulties during migration
    b. share self-consciousness and suffer disadvantages due to discrimination*
    c. share a physical trait that other people define as unique and different
    d. interact among each other for long periods of time and segregate themselves from others

4. In the chapter, it was explained that the classification systems many people use to divide all human beings into various racial categories are based on
    a. the social meanings assigned by people to certain biological characteristics*
    b. objectively identifiable genetic differences between groups of people
    c. unchanging statistical differences between groups of people in particular gene pools
    d. patterns of intermarriage within groups of people who have similar physical characteristics

5. From the material in the opening sections of the chapter, it could be concluded that the classification systems used to distinguish races
    a. generally identify three major races
    b. are the same in every major culture around the world
    c. are arbitrary systems based on continuous rather than discrete traits*
    d. have been based on genetic traits that influence behavior patterns

6. The author notes that recent research done by biologists and geneticists clearly shows that
    a. race has no biological validity in science*
    b. people in different races have many deep biological differences
    c. popular racial classification systems match findings in genetic research
    d. race is more scientific and biological than it is social or cultural

7. According to the author, attempts to use skin color to explain performance records across many different sports
    a. should be taken seriously in all scientific disciplines
    b. are a waste of research time and energy*
    c. have been used to challenge traditional ideas about race
    d. have been used to explain why downhill skiers are white

8. The author argues (in the boxed section) that when people use skin color to explain the achievements of black athletes, there is a tendency for them to forget the fact that
    a. the success of Swiss skiers is due to genetic advantages enjoyed by people who have white skin
    b. skilled dark-skinned athletes have many different individual physical attributes*
    c. selective breeding occurred as much among white-skinned people as it did among dark-skinned people during the 18th and 19th centuries
    d. white-skinned athletes have overcome genetic weaknesses through hard work

9. The author hypothesizes (in the boxed section) that the dominant racial ideology in the U.S. may influence athletic performance among black American men because it encourages those men
    a. to feel a powerful sense of biological and cultural destiny to become great athletes in certain sports*
    b. to have extremely high levels of self-confidence in all realms of social life
    c. to ignore high-paying, high-status opportunities in nonsport job categories
    d. to believe in the American Dream and in the notion that they should be all they can be

10. The author concludes (in the boxed section) that dominant race logic and racial ideology in the U.S. and many other countries has encouraged people to
    a. ignore the achievements of dark-skinned athletes in high-profile sports
    b. study the unique experiences of the ancestors of outstanding white volleyball players from California
    c. overlook the diversity of traits, backgrounds, and athletic achievements among people of color around the world*
    d. expect dark-skinned people from India and the Persian gulf to win more than their share of Olympic medals

11. The author explains that during the time when European peoples were colonizing many areas of the globe, they developed forms of "race logic" (or "racial theories") that enabled them to conclude that
   a. white-skinned people were superior and deserved to be in positions of power around the world*
   b. dark-skinned people were to be protected because they had formed cultures predating the cultures formed by light-skinned peoples
   c. dark-skinned people were intellectually superior but physically inferior to light skinned people
   d. people from cold-weather climates often had more physical strength than people from warm climates

12. The "race logic" used widely by white Europeans in the United States served as a basis for their explanations of performances of African American athletes. For example, when Joe Louis won the heavyweight boxing championship in 1935, many white sports journalists attributed his victory to
   a. his white manager and trainer, who had guided Louis' development as a boxer
   b. the nationalist support he received from the American people
   c. his animal-like and instinctive characteristics tied to his racial heritage*
   d. a work ethic grounded in his family background and his personal dedication to success as an athlete

13. According to the author, one of the reasons why the fictional character of Tarzan became popular in England and North America during the first half of this century was that
   a. black Africans held significant international political power held at that time
   b. many whites feared they were really not superior to people of color*
   c. Tarzan stories highlighted the inner spirit of people of color
   d. Tarzan stories challenged the entire notion of race and racial difference

14. The author notes that the existence of race logic in sports today is much more subtle than it was in the past. To make this point, the author explains that many people around the world explain the emergence and success of Kenyan and Ethiopian runners (nearly all men up to this point) in terms of
   a. the cultural experiences of east Africans who live in mountainous terrains
   b. the abilities of the whites who coach these runners
   c. the race-based genetic characteristics of the runners*
   d. the tendency of all dark-skinned peoples to work harder than white-skinned people

15. The author points out that race logic and gender logic are interconnected in sports. In his discussion of this point, he notes that black male athletes have become valuable entertainment commodities in sports emphasizing power and domination because
    a.   many people fear the power of black male bodies and are fascinated with their movements*
    b.   black men have been segregated in schools emphasizing certain sports
    c.   whites have simply refused to compete with blacks in most power sports
    d.   black men have learned special psychological techniques for dealing with the anxiety associated with sports

16. Sociologist Richard Majors has suggested that "cool pose" has become a patterned part of the lives of many black men in the United States. According to Majors,
    a.   those who use cool pose are usually those who have special physical skills to begin with
    b.   black mothers teach their sons to use cool pose so they will be successful in school
    c.   cool pose is most common among successful black professionals in law and medicine
    d.   cool pose involves an emphasis on being in control, being tough, and being detached from others*

17. Race logic in the U.S. and certain other societies has led to what has been described as "racial stacking." Racial stacking occurs when players from a certain racial or ethnic group are
    a.   excluded from certain sports and encouraged to play others
    b.   over-represented or under-represented in certain positions in team sports*
    c.   trained to play positions where injury rates are very high
    d.   encouraged to play individual rather than team sports

18. According to prevalent stacking patterns in U.S. sports, which of the following positions in major league baseball is most likely to be played by a black athlete?
    a.   shortstop
    b.   pitcher
    c.   third base
    d.   center field*

19. According to prevalent stacking patterns in U.S. sports, which of the following positions in professional football is most likely to be played by a black athlete?
    a.   offensive lineman
    b.   linebacker
    c.   defensive back*
    d.   tight end

20. Research has consistently shown that black athletes in professional football and baseball are most likely to play positions compatible with
   a.   the biological attributes of the black race as a whole
   b.   psychological orientations learned through socialization
   c.   racial and ethnic stereotypes used in the position assignment process*
   d.   the financial resources of those who own or sponsor teams

21. Research clearly indicates that racial and ethnic stacking exists
   a.   only in the U.S. and Canada
   b.   only in the major team sports in North America
   c.   in every country where slavery was once defined as legal
   d.   in many countries and in many sports*

22. The author notes that coaches and managers in team sports are frequently former athletes who played what people define as the thinking and dependability positions in those sports. In the past, this meant that former athletes most likely to be hired as coaches were
   a.   those who set performance records
   b.   mixed race
   c.   black
   d.   white*

23. Research shows that when blacks or Latinos have been hired in U.S. professional sports, they
   a.   were more likely than whites to get head coaching jobs without ever having served as assistant coaches
   b.   lost more games than white coaches did
   c.   have had longer and more productive careers as players than whites hired as coaches*
   d.   were more likely than white coaches to have close personal relationships with team owners

24. Information on the sport participation patterns of African Americans indicates that they
   a.   have come to make up more than half of all professional and amateur athletes in the U.S.
   b.   remain underrepresented in the majority of pro and amateur sports*
   c.   have not experienced racial segregation in sports since the years immediately following the Civil War
   d.   have always received better media press coverage than white athletes

25. The author notes that sport participation rates in the U.S. are highest in
   a.   low-income black communities
   b.   racially mixed communities regardless of family income in the communities
   c.   middle- and upper-middle income white communities*
   d.   low-income communities regardless of their racial makeup

26. The author notes that sport participation among Native Americans is limited due to poverty, poor health, a lack of equipment and facilities, and fears among Native Americans that becoming involved in sports will
    a. lead to serious injuries that will interfere with occupational success
    b. violate ancient religious traditions taught to them by their parents and in their schools
    c. lead to conflict between themselves and other minority athletes on their teams
    d. cut them off from their cultural roots and support systems for their identities*

27. In his discussion of the use of team nicknames and mascots based on images of Native Americans, the author makes the case (in the boxed section) that
    a. the use of names like "Chief" and "Savages" increases pride among native peoples
    b. when team mascots are dressed up in warpaint and war bonnets, white students develop more respect for native peoples
    c. the use of caricatures and stereotypes of Native Americans contributes to misunderstandings and racism*
    d. using the name "Redskins" is only justifiable when it is chosen with good intentions

28. The author suggests that when schools use names or symbols referring to Native Americans, they should do three things. Which of the following is *not* one of the things recommended by the author?
    a. send out regular press releases that provide information about the native peoples honored by the name or symbol
    b. sponsor ceremonies to inform students and parents about the people honored by names or symbols
    c. develop curricula and tests to make students more knowledgeable about the people honored by names or symbols
    d. encourage students to wear during games items sacred to the people honored by names or symbols*

29. According to the author, the sport participation patterns of Hispanics in North American is at least partly influenced by stereotypes and racial ideologies. The impact of these ethnic stereotypes is difficult to determine because the stereotypes are
    a. diverse and confusing*
    b. the same for different Latino groups
    c. expressed in behavior
    d. used only by African Americans and Native Americans

98

30. Anthropologist Doug Foley studied sports and intergroup relations (among other things) in a small Texas town. In his study, he noted that the Mexicano coach of the football team resigned in frustration because he could not
    a.   motivate Mexicano players unless he gave them special treatment
    b.   challenge bigotry and still meet the expectations of powerful Anglo boosters and school board members*
    c.   recruit the best athletes from a largely Anglo student body
    d.   convince the school board he deserved a raise after a very successful season

31. The author suggests that Latino involvement in U.S. sports will receive increased attention in the future because
    a.   Hispanics tend to live primarily in the midwest where people have strong interests in sports
    b.   all Latinos have a fanatical attachment to sports like football and basketball
    c.   young Latinos dominate high-school sports in most sections of the U.S. today
    d.   Hispanics are the fastest growing ethnic population in the U.S.*

32. The author points out that the sport participation of Asian Americans
    a.   varies with the genetic characteristics of the Asian group in question
    b.   differs depending on the specific histories of the different groups with Asian ancestry*
    c.   is limited to only two or three sports because Asian Americans are such a homogeneous group
    d.   is low because there is little motivation among Asian Americans to excel in competitive activities

33. In Mark Grey's study of high school sports and intergroup relations in a Kansas town, he discovered that when students from Asian immigrant families did not participate in school sports
    a.   their families were harassed until many decided to leave the town
    b.   they were socially marginalized in school and the community*
    c.   the school developed new sports related to their interests
    d.   they tended to become involved in more academically oriented activities where they were socially accepted

34. In the chapter it was pointed out that sport teams have four characteristics that often make them different from other organizational contexts when it comes to racial desegregation. Which of the following was *not* included among those four characteristics?
   a. the achievements of individual players on teams bring payoffs to other team members
   b. superior performances do not lead to promotions in the organizational structure of a sport
   c. the success of sport teams does not depend on teammates being friends with one another
   d. the people attracted to sport participation have fewer prejudices than people in other settings*

35. According to the author's conclusion, the desegregation of sports in the U.S. has been motivated strongly by
   a. financial profits*
   b. federal legislation
   c. the liberal attitudes of sport team owners
   d. political pressure coming from the black community

36. The racial desegregation of sports is related to the development of sport skills among blacks. Blacks have developed high level skills in certain sports, especially those which
   a. open up opportunities for them to interact with whites in informal social settings
   b. require the use of equipment combined with manual dexterity
   c. can be learned without the use of expensive equipment and facilities*
   d. involve contacts with people in the business community who can serve as sponsors for individuals and teams

37. According to the author, desegregation has been least likely to occur in sports involving
   a. extensive off-the-field social contact*
   b. high salaries for athletes at the professional level
   c. teamwork combined with complex strategies
   d. heavy media attention and widespread national publicity

38. Research on race relations has shown that contact between the people from different racial or ethnic groups is most likely to lead to favorable changes in attitudes when members of each group
   a. behave in conformity with stereotypes
   b. depend on one another's cooperation to achieve their goals*
   c. pursue different goals in separate but similar activities
   d. compete against each other in groups composed of members of the same racial or ethnic group

39. There are a number of reasons to be cautious in making the conclusion that sport brings the races together in ways that reduce racial prejudices. Which of the following is *not* one of the reasons given in the text?
    a. competition may aggravate existing prejudices
    b. interracial attitudes are very resistant to change
    c. the interracial contact in sport is often superficial and impersonal
    d. most coaches use racism to increase the motivation of both black and white players*

40. Research shows that when people are exposed to information that clearly challenges the racial ideologies that they have used throughout their lives, they often
    a. abandon their ideologies in favor of other explanations of how the world should and does work
    b. reinterpret the information so it fits with their ideologies*
    c. revise their ideologies to fit their new experiences
    d. seek out new friends and associates who assist them in seeing the world in new ways

41. Research suggests that the relationships between teammates from different racial or ethnic groups
    a. do not usually carry over into their personal, nonsport lives when there are pressures to maintain segregated relationships*
    b. usually become closer and more intimate when coaches loosen players up by telling racial and ethnic jokes
    c. are most problematic when members of a single minority group make up the majority of team members
    d. usually leads to intergroup dating patterns that cause problems in the community as a whole

42. When athletes from different racial or ethnic groups are opponents in games, meets, or matches, sports often become sites for
    a. abandoning negative stereotypes and seeking out new ways of relating to each other
    b. reproducing negative ideas about race and ethnicity*
    c. unlearning racist attitudes and concentrating on winning
    d. seeking opportunities to seriously injure their opponents

43. According to the author, sports are most likely to become sites for the improvement of intergroup relations when
    a. those who control sports get together and challenge dominant racial ideologies*
    b. everyone involved in sports ignores racial and ethnic differences
    c. coaches and athletes focus all their attention on doing the best they can
    d. the media refuse to cover any issues that expose negative attitudes and behaviors

44. As described in the chapter, Project TEAMWORK is a program through which students
    a. assist the police in arresting troublemakers in schools
    b. work with teachers to develop courses on intergroup relations
    c. are trained to work in groups to monitor intergroup relations and intervene when problems exist*
    d. evaluate their peers' attitudes and turn in those who do not conform to correct ways of behaving

45. The author recommends that sport programs in high schools and colleges should involve athletic directors, coaches, trainers, and athletes in
    a. biofeedback training so people can control their own thoughts more effectively
    b. behavior modification exercises in which people are rewarded for doing kind things for others
    c. teamwork training sessions that emphasize the need for cooperation within groups
    d. diversity training sessions that critically examine the dominant racial ideology in the society*

ESSAY QUESTIONS

1. Recent research in biology and genetics has led to the conclusion that the concept of race has no biological validity. Explain what this means and why it is so difficult for many people to accept.

2. A biologist at Yale University has recently stated: "Race has no biological reality. The human species simply does not come packaged that way." But some people continue to mistakenly use "race" to categorize people into what they claim are biologically distinct groups. They do not understand that "race" is a social concept grounded in the social meanings people attach to specific physical traits. Why have people chosen skin color as a socially meaningful trait, and what are the difficulties in using skin color to classify all the people of the world into races? What do these new discoveries about "race" mean when it comes to using "race" to explain performance in sports?

3. The "race logic" that underlies dominant racial ideology in the U.S. has had a powerful impact on the way people think about potential and achievement. How has race logic influenced what has happened in the world of sports when it comes to opportunities to participate and the way people explain the achievements of athletes, both dark- and light-skinned?

4.   After you and some friends watch the men's semi-final matches during the Wimbledon Tennis Championships, one of your friends says "I wonder why there are so few black tennis players - it must be something biological." You tell your friend that there are a number of nonbiological explanations for why there are so few black tennis players. He asks you to name four of them. What would you say in return?

5.   The author argues that in U.S. history, black male bodies have been "seen" differently than black female bodies or the bodies of white men and women. This has led to a situation where some black men exhibit what might be called "cool pose" and where many black male athletes have become valuable entertainment commodities. How does the author support this argument, and do you agree or disagree with it. Explain your position.

6.   The author provides a sociological explanation for the performance of African Americans in certain sports. He argues that the notable achievements of African Americans in certain sports are due in part to a powerful sense of cultural and biological destiny that many young blacks, especially males, use to inform their decisions about what to do with their lives. Explain the origins of this hypothesized sense of destiny and indicate if you agree or disagree with the theory.

7.   During the fall semester, you have watched a number of U.S. pro football games with students from outside the U.S. Toward the end of the season, one of the students asks you why she seldom sees black quarterbacks and why most of the running backs and pass receivers are black. How would you explain this pattern to her?

8.   Discrimination usually tends to be self-perpetuating. Show how this is true by showing how stacking patterns in football and baseball have implications for who is most likely to get coaching jobs in those sports.

9.   Your son is attending a school whose nickname for its sport teams is the "Redskins." The mascot is a caricature of a Native American in war paint and war bonnet carrying a tomahawk in one hand and a spear in the other. The assistant principal asks your son to be the mascot for the upcoming season. Your son thinks this would be an honor, and he asks you if you approve. You tell him that you have serious questions about whether he should do it. He wants to know why. What do you tell him?

10.   You are a principal of a high school in a major urban area. Your school's nickname is "Indians" and the school's mascot is a caricature of a male Indian in warpaint and eagle feathers doing a dance and singing a chant. A group of Native Americans from the local area comes to you and tells you they are very offended by the caricature and the lack of respect your logo shows for their religious beliefs; they ask that you drop the name, logo, and team cheers that mimic Indian religious songs. Explain what might be done in response to this request.

11. Ethnic stereotypes sometimes influence people's perceptions and expectations when it comes to athletic ability. How have stereotypes about Latinos in general and Mexicans in particular influenced ideas about ability and sport participation?

12. Your town has recently had a large influx of immigrants from Mexico and a few Asian countries. The editor of your local newspaper writes an editorial in which he suggests that the high school's varsity sport program is an effective tool for establishing good intergroup relations in the town. You read it and conclude he is not aware of research on this topic and how difficult it is to use sports in this way. You write a letter to the editor in which you explain these things to the readers of the paper. What does your letter say?

13. Over your Christmas break, you are watching a professional basketball game with your father. During the game, he mentions that the majority of players on both teams are black. In commenting on this, he says that blacks have always received fair treatment in American sports despite discrimination in other areas. How would you tell your father that this is not the case? What information would you use to back up your statements as you talk with him?

14. After you have convinced your father that desegregation in sport is only a recent phenomenon, he asks you to explain why sports have higher proportions of blacks than there are in other types of business organizations. How would you explain to him that sport is a unique context when it comes to racial desegregation?

15. The phrase "money talks" seems to be quite relevant when explaining the desegregation of sport in the U.S. Explain what this means. How have financial considerations influenced decisions about desegregation?

16. Many people have referred to basketball as "the city game." Why is basketball referred to in this way? In your discussion of this question, explain why there are so many black high school students with highly developed basketball skills?

17. You are a teacher in an inner-city school with a student body that is 90% black. After a big basketball game in which your school's team defeated an all-white team from a suburban school, you notice an increase in anti-white feelings among your students. How would you explain this phenomenon to another teacher who says that he thought sport always created brotherhood between the races?

18. As a football coach at an integrated school, you notice that your black players get along with your white players just fine on the field, but their off-the-field social activities are largely segregated. How would you explain this and what could you do to change this pattern?

19. Project TEAMWORK has been developed by people concerned with improving intergroup relations in U.S. high schools. Explain how the project works and whether it would work in your old high school (or a local high school). How would you change Project TEAMWORK to make it more effective?

CHAPTER 10
SOCIAL CLASS:
does economic inequality matter in sports?

CHAPTER OUTLINE

I. Sports and economic inequality
    A. The dynamics of class relations
    B. Class relations and who has the power in sports
    C. Sports as a vehicle for transferring public money to the private sector

II. Social class and sport participation patterns
    A. Homemaking, child-rearing, and earning a living: what happens when class and gender relations come together in women's lives?
    B. Getting respect and becoming a man: what happens when class and gender relations come together in men's lives?
    C. Fighting to survive: what happens when class, gender, and race and ethnic relations come together?
    D. Class relations in action: the decline of high school sports in low-income areas
    E. The cost of attending sport events

III. Opportunities in sports: myth and reality
    A. Opportunities are limited and short term
    B. Opportunities for women are limited
    (BOX, "Women's professional basketball in the U.S.: will it succeed?")
    C. Opportunities for African Americans are limited
        1. Employment barriers for black athletes
        2. Employment barriers in coaching and off-the-field jobs in sports

IV. Sport participation and occupational careers among former athletes
    A. Sport participation, class relations, and career success
    B. Highly paid professional athletes and occupational success
        1. When does retirement from sports present problems?
    C. Athletic grants and occupational success

V. Conclusion: are sports related to economic inequality and social mobility in sports?

MULTIPLE CHOICE QUESTIONS

1. Sport participation through history has been closely related to patterns of social stratification in all societies. This is because a formally organized, institutionalized activity, including sports, depends on
   a. the endorsements of the majority of the middle class
   b. high literacy rates among participants
   c. written forms of communication and an understanding of written rules
   d. the availability of resources*

2. The author makes the point that sports are tied to class relations in any society. This means that sports are generally defined, organized, and played in ways that
   a. bring people from different social classes together
   b. fit the interests of those who have money and power in society*
   c. promote democracy and political participation throughout all social classes
   d. give low-income people as many participation opportunities as people from elite groups

3. According to the author's example of how age relations operate in sports, the organization of youth sport programs generally reflects
   a. what adults think children should be doing and learning in sports*
   b. the needs of children and their interests in action and personal involvement
   c. the types of sports that are not sponsored by schools
   d. managerial approaches used by adults in major corporations

4. The author argues that when sports in a society are tied to an ideology that stresses material achievement and the belief that success is based on the ability to compete against and outscore opponents, they tend to
   a. lead people to ridicule wealthy people and their indulgent lifestyles
   b. promote high amounts of worker productivity and satisfaction
   c. contribute to the preservation of the power and influence of elite groups in society*
   d. enable people from low-income groups to challenge the power of those who are economically successful

5. According to the author, the "class logic" underlying dominant sport forms in North America involve the belief that
   a. you get what you deserve and you deserve what you get*
   b. money isn't everything
   c. being a professional is always better than being an amateur
   d. its better to be lucky than hard working or smart

6. According to the author many people in North America *mistakenly* believe that sports are models of
   a. hard work
   b. luck and good fortune
   c. competition
   d. social equality*

7. According to *The Sporting News* list of the 100 Most Powerful People in Sports during 1996, the people at the very top of the list were primarily
   a. high profile athletes
   b. CEOs of transnational media companies*
   c. coaches who were also team owners
   d. wealthy owners of professional sport teams

8. The author argues that the images and messages emphasized in the media coverage of sports tend to represent the interests of those who are the primary sponsors of media sports. At this point in time, the primary sponsors are
   a. women's organizations advocating changes in gender relations around the world
   b. labor unions and other organizations representing the interests of workers
   c. large, transnational corporations with interests in capitalist expansion*
   d. environmental groups who lobby against unregulated capitalist expansion around the world

9. The author argues that those who become the primary providers of popular pleasure and entertainment in society can use that pleasure and entertainment as vehicles to
   a. deliver other messages about what should be important in people's lives*
   b. help people around the world gain control over their lives
   c. deliver subliminal messages that determine what people think
   d. maintain a global corporate conspiracy to undermine democratic governments

10. The author argues that because of the dynamics of class relations in the U.S., sports have become a means for
   a. transferring public money to wealthy individuals and corporations in the private sector*
   b. efficiently and cheaply creating jobs benefitting people from the working class
   c. making social changes that have opened doors for women and minorities in the ranks of top corporate officials
   d. strategically destroying real estate values in large areas of major cities

11. Research on sport participation and social class tends to show that
    a. high-income people watch more sports, but low-income people play more sports
    b. low-income people cannot afford to play or watch most sports
    c. high-income people have the highest rates of participation and attendance at most sport events*
    d. participation in sports that promote physical fitness is highest among those who do physical labor in their jobs

12. The author points out that the lifestyles of low- and middle-income people are most likely to include those sports that have traditionally been
    a. free, open, and sponsored with public funds*
    b. physical, aggressive and sometimes violent
    c. family-oriented and played indoors
    d. highly competitive and played outdoors

13. According to the author, gender relations and class relations often come together in a way that enables some women to have higher sport participation rates than other women. The category of women with the highest participation rate is
    a. women from low-income households
    b. women from upper-income households*
    c. women who work outside the home
    d. women with active children

14. Being married and having children is most likely to interfere with the sport participation of women
    a. in upper-income families
    b. who have wealthy friends
    c. who have husbands working at home
    d. in lower-income families*

15. Mike Messner's research (summarized in the chapter) on men who had been elite athletes led him to conclude that males from lower-income backgrounds were more likely than their higher-income counterparts to see sport participation mainly as a means of obtaining
    a. acceptance by their parents
    b. job skills that could be used if they did not attend college
    c. respect and a foundation for their identities*
    d. the material things that other young people had

16. The author uses quotes from people interviewed by sociologist Loic Wacquant to make the point that participation in professional boxing is best understood in terms of
    a. the personalities of those who choose to box
    b. the social context in which people make choices about their lives*
    c. the large salaries made by nearly all professional boxers
    d. how and why fathers who box encourage their children to be boxers

17. In his research on boxers, French sociologist Loic Wacquant notes that being a professional boxer in the U.S. is a life choice
    a. leading many men into gang cultures
    b. made before a male is 10 years old
    c. influenced by racial and class necessity*
    d. indicating a rejection of available educational opportunities

18. According to the author, an increasing number of high school sport programs are being cut in the U.S. These cuts occur most often in communities where there are
    a. many private sport programs for young people
    b. problems with public mass transportation
    c. large corporations willing take over the funding of all school sports
    d. large proportions of low-income families*

19. According to data on average ticket prices at men's professional sports in North America, the recent pattern has been for ticket prices to
    a. increase faster than the rate of inflation*
    b. stay about the same if inflation is taken into account
    c. decline significantly to attract middle-income families
    d. be rigidly controlled by city governments that fund stadiums

20. The author argues that efforts to organize fans will
    a. succeed because fans increasingly represent union workers who are committed to protesting unfair pricing policies
    b. fail because fans want to make sure that stadium employees are well paid
    c. fail because status-conscious season ticket holders do not have an interest in lowering the cost of tickets*
    d. succeed because many season ticket holders want to eliminate class distinctions among spectators

21. There are many different ways to compute the odds for making it to certain levels in sports. After looking at the data presented in the chapter, it could be concluded that
    a. African American males have a better chance of playing in the NBA than in the NFL
    b. 15 to 39 year old men in the U.S. have about a 20,000 to 1 chance of being pro athletes in the top pro leagues*
    c. the odds of becoming a pro in individual sports are much better than they are in team sports
    d. women have much better chances of becoming pro athletes than men have

22. After the author reviews data on the odds of playing professional sports, he concludes that opportunities for making it to the top as an athlete are
    a. increasing now that teams recruit players from all over the world
    b. better than the odds of becoming a doctor or lawyer
    c. better for Hispanics than any other ethnic group
    d. extremely limited for men and women from all ethnic backgrounds*

23. Players who sign contracts in major North American team sports are usually about 22 years old. According to data presented in the chapter, this means that they will face retirement from their playing careers between the ages of
    a. 24 and 26 years old
    b. 28 and 32 years old
    c. 26 and 30 years old*
    d. 32 and 45 years old

24. In the boxed section on women's professional basketball in the U.S., the author notes that
    a. during the first year of the ABL, players had average salaries of $70,000*
    b. women's salaries in the WNBA were nearly as high as the average salaries in the NBA when the WNBA first began
    c. during their first year of operation, the two women's pro leagues provided paid opportunities for over 1000 women athletes
    d. women's professional team sports did not exist in the U.S. prior to 1990

25. According to the prevailing gender logic in the athletic departments of many colleges and universities, salaries are likely to be lowest among
    a. both men and women who coach men's teams
    b. only women who coach men's teams
    c. both men and women who coach women's teams*
    d. only men who coach women's teams

26. Career opportunities for women in sports have traditionally been very limited. However, the author notes that increases in opportunities can be expected
    a. in jobs such as public relations and marketing*
    b. head coaching and top administration jobs in all sports
    c. in men's sports programs, especially at large universities
    d. in officiating jobs such as referees and umpires

27. The author argues that women who work in sport organizations often face the burden of
    a. doing jobs for which they have few skills
    b. working for women supervisors who were hired because of the traditional gender logic used in those organizations
    c. being promoted into athletic director positions before they are ready
    d. not having been involved in shaping the organizational culture where they work*

28. According to the author's analysis, women are less likely to get certain jobs in sports and sport organizations because being qualified for these jobs is
    a. often defined as being able to do them as men have done them in the past*
    b. dependent on having a deep knowledge of sports
    c. related to accomplishments and awards received as an athlete
    d. usually related to how one is evaluated by athletes

29. The author argues that full gender equity in jobs in sport organizations depends on
    a. women developing alliances with powerful men in sports
    b. changing the cultures of sports and sport organizations*
    c. women working harder to learn what sport organizations do
    d. dropping affirmative action and using truly objective criteria to assess job qualifications

30. After reviewing data on opportunities for African Americans in sports, the author concludes that opportunities for African Americans in sports are
    a. more scarce in team sports than in individual sports
    b. greater than they are in traditional professions such as medicine and law
    c. so few that they are insignificant for the African American population as a whole*
    d. more plentiful for African American women than for men

31. According to the author, the belief among young African Americans that sports are the best way to achieve upward social mobility will continue to exist as long as
    a. young African Americans do not perceive opportunities in other careers*
    b. a large proportion of African American families live in large urban areas
    c. colleges and universities continue to give athletic scholarships
    d. there are so many jobs for African Americans in professional sports

32. When sports were first desegregated, the existence of "entry barriers" in top-level competitive sports in the U.S. created a situation in which
    a. white athletes were always the best players on integrated teams
    b. black athletes sat on the bench more than they played
    c. black athletes had better performance records than white athletes*
    d. black athletes received higher salaries than white athletes

33. Richard Lapchick's analysis of data from the NBA between 1960 and the late-1970s, and Paul Kooistra's data from the NFL in the early 1990s, showed the existence of
    a. retention barriers that favored black players with good potential
    b. contract favoritism for white players with top performance records
    c. contract barriers that favored black players with seniority in the league
    d. retention barriers that favored white players with marginal skills*

34. The author reports that data on the salaries of players in the major teams sports shows that
    a. white players make less than players from ethnic minorities
    b. there is no evidence of race-based salary discrimination*
    c. black players make less than white players
    d. salaries in team sports are influenced by race, but this is not the case in individual sports

35. Information on the number of blacks in coaching, staff, and management positions in North American professional team sports shows that
   a.   at least 30% of these positions are held by blacks
   b.   blacks hold the majority of coaching positions only in basketball
   c.   blacks are underrepresented in most positions in all sports*
   d.   the majority of all assistant coaches in most sports are black

36. According to the author's analysis, affirmative action programs have not led to significant increases in the proportions of blacks working at top management levels in sports because
   a.   talented blacks choose to take non-sport jobs
   b.   the dynamics of hiring people in top jobs favor those with characteristics similar to team owners*
   c.   white males are threatened by qualified blacks, especially when the blacks have been outstanding athletes
   d.   team owners fear that ticket sales will decline if fans see blacks in top positions

37. Studies comparing the career patterns of young people from comparable backgrounds who played varsity sports while they were in high school and those who did not play varsity sports have generally shown that former athletes as a group
   a.   have a clear record of higher occupational achievement than others
   b.   have a poorer record of occupational achievement than others
   c.   have career patterns that start slow but end up more successful than others
   d.   have no more or less career success than others*

38. After the author reviewed studies on the social mobility of athletes, he concluded that being a varsity athlete in high school or college is most likely to give people an occupational advantage when
   a.   their parents had the resources to help them focus attention on becoming the best athletes they could be
   b.   they were good enough to set records and have everyone recognize them as athletes
   c.   sport participation enabled them to expand their relationships and experiences outside of sports*
   d.   their experiences were defined as fulfilling and satisfying after they retired from competitive sports

39. According to the analysis in the text, the potential for future career success would be highest among former elite athletes who had participated in
   a.   golf*
   b.   track and field
   c.   boxing
   d.   rodeo

40. Mike Messner's interviews with former top-level athletes led him to conclude that there were two major challenges associated with retiring from sports. One challenge was reconstructing their identities, and the other was
    a. finding jobs that would help them avoid poverty
    b. recovering from the emotional shock of not being a public figure anymore
    c. finding new ways to stay involved in sports
    d. renegotiating their relationships with family and friends*

41. After reviewing information on "retirement from sport," the author concludes that most athletes do not have serious problems when they stop playing sports at top levels of competition. Problems are more likely when retirement
    a. is forced on an athlete because of injury*
    b. comes in connection with other life changes
    c. is related to a loss of skills that comes with age
    d. forces a person to develop interests outside of sports

42. In his discussion of retirement from competitive sports, the author notes that there is a growing belief that sport organizations should
    a. not "cut" athletes and should have policies that all retirements by athletes be voluntary
    b. assist athletes during their transition into other parts of their lives*
    c. set up special teams to enable "senior" athletes to continue competing
    d. hire all former athletes back in some coaching or administrative capacity

43. In the discussion of athletic grants/scholarships and occupational success, the author presents data indicating that
    a. less than 25% of the student athletes with athletic grants in universities with big-time sport programs have full scholarships*
    b. in the largest universities in the U.S., over 10% of all students receive some form of athletic aid
    c. athletic scholarships have a major impact on the career success and upward social mobility of at least 30% of all college students
    d. more students receive athletic scholarships than is popularly believed

44. After reading the chapter on social class and sports, it is clear that in recent years
    a. women and ethnic minorities have taken over most sports and sport organizations
    b. affirmative action has changed who obtains jobs in top management positions in sports and sport organizations
    c. white men have retained their power and control as well as the majority of good jobs in sport organizations*
    d. government involvement in sports has caused white males to lose much of their power in sports and sport organizations

113

ESSAY QUESTIONS

1. You are a bartender in an exclusive downtown athletic club. After a game of squash, two white male executives sit down at your bar and talk about the recent NBA playoffs. They both agree that sports is one of the only spheres of life that does not reflect the social inequality that exists in the rest of society. They praise sports because they are truly democratic and open to everyone. They ask if you agree. How do you respond?

2. High-profile, organized sports are now presented in a way that reinforces an ideology of individual achievement. In other words, sports promote a particular form of class logic that works to the advantage of some people and the disadvantage of others. Explain how this class logic is reproduced through dominant forms of sports and provide examples of who benefits and who does not benefit from this class logic.

3. According to the list published by *The Sporting News* in the U.S., who are the most powerful people in sports today, and why are no coaches or athletes on the list? What are the characteristics of the most powerful people in sports, and what interests do they represent as they make decisions about sports?

4. The author argues that sport-participation patterns, including attendance at sport events, can be explained largely in terms of class relations in society. Explain how social class is related to sport participation and give examples of this relationship from your personal experiences or the experiences of people you know.

5. Explain how class relations and gender relations might overlap when it comes to the sport-participation patterns of the following two women: both women have equal physical skills and equal interests in sports; both have three children, one at home, one in pre-school for half days, and one in third grade. Neither woman works outside the home; the husband of one makes about $23,000 as a car mechanic, the husband of the other makes $80,000 as a sales representative for a pharmaceutical company. Explain why these two women would probably have completely different sport-participation patterns in their lives.

6. Boxing gyms are most often located in low-income, predominantly minority neighborhoods; they are never located in high-income neighborhoods where people with established wealthy live. Why is this the case? In your essay, explain why participation in boxing is best explained in terms of a combination of class, gender, and ethnic relations in society.

7. When children say they want to be professional athletes when they grow up, they don't understand that athletic careers in pro sports are very different than other types of careers. What are some of the major differences, and what should children be told about their chances of playing professional sports?

8.   When people talk about opportunities in sports they are generally referring to opportunities for males. What kinds of opportunities exist for women? Have these opportunities increased now that women's sport programs have increased in number and popularity?

9.   You are at a party with a group of friends. When the conversation turns to sports, one of them says that if it weren't for sports, blacks in the U.S. would be in much worse shape (socioeconomically) than they are now. He continues by saying that being a good athlete is still "the best way out of the ghetto" for young African Americans. How would you respond to these comments? Would you agree or disagree, and what would you say to back up your position?

10.   Breaking into top sport management jobs has been slow for women and minorities. One of your friends says this is due to a lack of qualified candidates; another says it is due to the fears of whites. Explain to your friends there is another interpretation, and then explain this alternative interpretation so they will understand.

11.   It is popularly believed that all those who become athletes in top-level competitive sports in American society will have no trouble being successful in careers after they retire from active sport participation. Do you agree with this popular belief? What factors are related to career success and mobility for these former athletes?

12.   Many adults in your city are very concerned about what they describe as a "youth gang problem." Their goal is to develop programs to deal with this problem in ways that will really help young people get the experiences they need to be occupationally successful in the future. One person on the city council suggests building a gym to house a boxing program. You are asked if this would be the correct approach. How would you respond and what would you say is needed for young people to use sport experiences as a means of upward social mobility?

13.   Using one of the men's and one of the women's varsity teams on your campus as an example, explain how the college experiences of team members may be related to career success and social mobility after they get out of school. What are the things that might contribute to success and mobility? What are the things that might interfere with success and mobility?

14.   Two of your friends are arguing. One says that former pro athletes have it made when they retire because they have ample money to have a good time and enjoy life; the other says that former athletes have serious problems in retirement because they have no skills and no real idea about what life is like outside of sports. Your job is to try to get each of these people to see things in ways that will lead them to continue to be friends. So what would you say as you entered their discussion? How would you try to get them to see things in a similar manner?

15.   Your parents are having a party during Christmas vacation. Some of the guests are talking about athletic scholarships in college. One of them says that athletic scholarships are great because they primarily serve to give poor kids a chance to attend college. After making the statement, the person looks at you and says, "Isn't that right?" What would you say in response? Explain who receives scholarships and how many scholarships are given to student-athletes.

16.   Your younger brother, a first-year student in high school, has just made the school's junior varsity team. Your father is very pleased and tells your brother that if he tries hard enough he will have a good chance of getting a scholarship to college and maybe even playing in the pros. Do you agree with what your father told your brother? What could you tell your father so he would be able to provide better and more realistic advice to your brother in the future?

CHAPTER 11
SPORTS AND THE ECONOMY:
what are the characteristics of commercial sports?

CHAPTER OUTLINE

I.   Emergence and growth of commercial sports
        A.   General conditions
        B.   Class relations and commercial sports
        C.   The creation of spectator interest in sports
                1.   Success ideology and spectator interest
                2.   Youth sport programs and spectator interest
                3.   Media coverage and spectator interest
        D.   Economic motives and the globalization of commercial sports
                1.   Sport organizations look for global markets
                2.   Corporations use sports as vehicles for global expansion
                3.   Outposts in action: beer and football

II.   Commercialization and changes in sports
        A.   Structure and goals
        B.   Orientations of players, coaches, and sponsors
        C.   Sport organizations

III.   Owners, sponsors, and promoters in commercial sports
        A.   Professional sports in North America
                1.   Team owners and sport leagues as monopolies
                2.   Team owners and forms of public assistance
                3.   Sources of income for team owners
        B.   Amateur sports in North America

IV.   Legal status and incomes of athletes in commercial sports
        A.   Professional athletes
                1.   Legal status: team sports
                2.   Legal status: individual sports
                3.   Income: team sports
                4.   Income: individual sports
                        a.   How much do athletes make on endorsements?
                        b.   Do athletes salaries affect ticket prices to sports events?
                        c.   Do big salaries influence the motivation of athletes?
        B.   Amateur athletes in commercial sports
                1.   Legal status of amateur athletes
                2.   Income of amateur athletes

V.   Conclusion: the characteristics of commercial sports

MULTIPLE CHOICE QUESTIONS

1. In the discussion of the general conditions underlying the emergence and growth of commercial sports, the author notes that the existence of commercial sports depends on their ability to
    a. attract the attention and support of powerful political and economic leaders
    b. generate revenues from gate receipts, sponsorships, and the sale of broadcasting rights*
    c. present fans with exciting but controlled forms of violence
    d. eliminate competition with other forms of entertainment

2. The author explains that commercial sports are most likely to grow and prosper in societies characterized by
    a. market economies, urbanization, and the availability of capital*
    b. high rates of unemployment combined with access to transportation
    c. traditional definitions of masculinity and femininity
    d. low rates of consumption and little awareness of status differences

3. The author argues that golf has become a major commercial sport in certain countries because those who are interested in golf
    a. tend to watch more television than other people in society
    b. have more free time than other people in society
    c. are more likely to be influenced by advertising messages than others in society
    d. have more economic resources and influence than others in society*

4. According to the author, football has become "America's game" because it
    a. fits with rural traditions and values in the heartland of the country
    b. meets the interests of people from all social backgrounds in the society
    c. celebrates and privileges the values and experiences of powerful people in the society*
    d. emphasizes democratic values and the notion that people always win when they try hard

5. Class relations are connected with commercial sports in any society because
    a. low-income people use sports to learn models of success in society
    b. people with economic resources in society promote and sponsor sports that fit their interests*
    c. commercial sports usually recruit athletes from low-income backgrounds
    d. people are always attracted to the sports played by people possessing power and wealth in society

118

6. Spectator interest in commercial sports is created and nurtured in connection with certain cultural conditions. Which of the following is *not* one of the three conditions discussed in the chapter?
    a. beliefs that there is a causal connection between success and hard work
    b. a widespread system of youth sport programs in which children learn to value sports and sport skills
    c. the existence of a large group of low-income male workers who have extra time on their hands*
    d. general access to the mass media, especially television

7. Television has had a positive impact on the growth of commercial sports. According to the author's explanation, its most important impact is that it
    a. distracts people's attention from physical activity in their own lives
    b. forces sports and sport teams to compete with each other for revenues
    c. builds strong rivalries between players on various teams in sport leagues
    d. serves as an effective tool for recruiting new spectators and fans*

8. According to the author's analysis, the globalization of commercial sports is due in part to the fact that
    a. sport organizations are interested in expanding their markets*
    b. athletes as a group like to travel to new places when playing sports
    c. airlines are one of the major corporate sponsors of professional sports around the world
    d. customs regulations have been eliminated or loosened up in many countries around the world

9. The author explains that corporations now use sports as vehicles for their own global expansion. The author then argues that large, transnational corporations sponsor sports because the corporations want to
    a. sell their products to athletes and coaches
    b. encourage people to spend more of their time away from work and in front of the television
    c. convince people that corporations and their products bring pleasure and enjoyment into people's lives*
    d. improve the health and well being of people around the world

10. According to sociologist Joe Maguire's analysis of the growth of American football in England, the Anheuser Busch corporation subsidized the first league because
    a. company officials wanted to hide the fact that they were buying large amounts of stock in British companies
    b. their profits on beer sales were so high they wanted to do something nice for British beer drinkers
    c. they knew that soccer was losing its popularity and British sport fans were looking for a new sport
    d. they wanted to change the image of lager beer in the minds of British men so the men would drink Budweiser beer*

119

11. The analysis in the chapter emphasizes that spectators are generally attracted to sports events in which there are high stakes, noteworthy performances by athletes, and
   a. uncertain outcomes*
   b. expensive ticket prices
   c. high rates of injuries
   d. few rules and regulations

12. In the author's analysis of the effects of commercialization on sports, it was concluded that commercialization has
   a. affected coaches much more than it has affected athletes
   b. produced dramatic changes in the basic structure and goals of most sports
   c. changed the orientations of players, coaches, and others connected with sports*
   d. eliminated much of the excitement associated with sports

13. The author notes that when rules are developed or changed in connection with commercialization, the new rules are likely to
   a. increase scoring*
   b. slow down the action
   c. encourage lopsided scores
   d. eliminate breaks in the action

14. The author explains that the orientations of athletes, coaches, and the promoters of sports are most likely to be affected by a certain characteristic of mass audiences. This characteristic is the audience's
   a. average social class background
   b. general willingness to view aggressive action
   c. average age and education level
   d. technical knowledge about a sport and sport skills*

15. The analysis of commercialization in the chapter suggests that in commercial sports there is a tendency for aesthetic values to be replaced by
   a. democratic values
   b. spectator values
   c. economic values
   d. heroic values*

16. After reading the analysis in the chapter, which of the following is most likely to be emphasized in commercial sports?
   a. the style and excitement of movement by athletes*
   b. the technical physical abilities of athletes
   c. the willingness of athletes to explore limits
   d. athletes' commitment to being involved in sports

17. According to the author, an indicator of the promotional culture that is created in connection with commercial sports is *USA Today's Olympic Advertising Index*. Which of the following is *not* one of the four scales used to evaluate athletes on the index?
    a. the on-camera appeal scale
    b. the maturity scale*
    c. the athletic ability scale
    d. the pizazz factor scale

18. When sports become commercialized, there are changes in the organizations controlling them. These changes involve shifts in
    a. who makes decisions and how those decisions reflect the interests of athletes*
    b. the leadership techniques used by those in management positions
    c. organizational accounting procedures and personnel policies
    d. the ways that referees are hired, fired, and assigned to events

19. Professional sports teams in North America are privately owned. Apart from the top professional franchises in North America, most people who own the hundreds of minor league teams
    a. show annual profits that make team ownership a wise investment
    b. regularly lose money on their investments*
    c. have decided to invest in sports because of the public subsidies that enable them to make money
    d. use local endorsements to make vast amounts of money

20. According to the author, the owners of sport teams and the sponsors of major sport events do not think alike on all issues but they generally
    a. love sports more than their own businesses
    b. agree on the need to protect their investments and maximize profits*
    c. come from similar backgrounds and attended similar types of colleges
    d. adhere to progressive and liberal political and economic ideologies

21. The franchise fees paid by the owners of new teams in the major men's sport leagues in North America have
    a. generally stayed the same except in football
    b. recently declined to their lowest amounts in history
    c. increased dramatically over the past three decades*
    d. declined in hockey but increased in the other three sports

22. League policies that specify the conditions under which new teams may enter North American professional men's sport leagues are designed primarily to
    a. prevent new teams from competing with existing teams for players and income*
    b. give as many people as possible the chance to own a professional team
    c. protect cities from new owners who might be greedy
    d. conform to a free market approach to business and economics

121

23. The relationships between the team owners in the major professional team sports in North America are most accurately described as forms of
    a. free enterprise competition
    b. legal monopolies*
    c. civic charity
    d. illegal trusts

24. Over the past 25 years the people who have bought and sold teams in the NBA, NFL, NHL, and Major League Baseball have
    a. lost money on the sale but made money on annual gate receipts
    b. used their popularity to begin political careers
    c. made money but lost most of it to taxes
    d. made vast amounts of money on the sale*

25. Professional sport team owners in the U.S. often receive public assistance in the form of
    a. donations from revenue sharing funds
    b. free public transportation for fans holding season tickets
    c. free parking for those who attend games
    d. tax breaks and subsidies related to the use of facilities*

26. The author explains that stadium subsidies and other forms of public support for professional sport teams have been justified through five major arguments. Which of the following is *not* one of those arguments?
    a. pro teams create positive psychic and social benefits
    b. a stadium and a pro team creates jobs
    c. pro teams share their profits with city governments*
    d. pro teams attract other businesses to the city

27. According to the research review done by the author, the arguments used to justify subsidies for pro sport teams are
    a. supported by studies done by all economists
    b. contradicted by studies done by both liberal and conservative independent economists*
    b. contradicted only by studies done by liberal economists
    c. supported by studies done by independent economists

28. After reviewing the arguments and counter arguments for spending public money to subsidize stadiums and pro sport team owners, the author concludes that
    a. subsidies are justified if team owners are truly needy
    b. the public good is served best if public money is spent on projects other than a stadium*
    c. sport fans with season tickets deserve to have public money used for their leisure-time enjoyment
    d. if cities lost pro sport teams, they would experience major economic recessions

29. According to the author, many pro sport team owners have made requests for new stadiums in recent years because they want to
    a. serve a greater number of the local citizens, especially those from working class backgrounds
    b. have the highest-paid players in their respective leagues
    c. hold down ticket prices for the average sport spectator
    d. profit from the sale of luxury suites and revenues from concessions and parking*

30. The nonprofit sponsors of amateur sports in the U.S. are primarily interested in
    a. maintaining their power and raising money through sponsorships*
    b. preserving the processes through which athletes are able to control their own careers in sport
    c. promoting amateur sports as vehicles to generate mass sport participation among people of all ages
    d. organizing competitions for young athletes in developmental programs

31. The power of the organizations which control amateur sports in the U.S. is primarily related to
    a. the number of their athletes who have successful careers outside of sports
    b. their relationships with political leaders and governmental agencies
    c. the amount of money they generate through sport events and sponsorships*
    d. the organizational abilities of their administrators

32. The author argues that as corporate sponsorships are used as the sole basis of support for amateur athletes and sport organizations, the economics of amateur sports will depend on
    a. the income earning potential of amateur athletes
    b. the business training of amateur sport officials
    c. the extent to which corporate executives see amateur sports contributing to the common good around the world
    d. the fortunes and fluctuations of market economies and the profits of large corporations*

33. The legal status of most athletes in professional team sports in North America has been governed in the past by what is called the *reserve system*. The reserve system has generally served to
    a. give players total control over their own careers
    b. increase the salaries of the best athletes
    c. give team owners an extreme degree of power over players*
    d. give wealthy team owners an advantage over other team owners

34. When changes in the legal status of athletes allow them to become "free agents," this means that the athletes are free to
   a.   sign a contract with any team they choose*
   b.   unite with other athletes to force owners to increase salaries
   c.   switch teams at the end of every season depending on who they want to play for
   d.   hire an agent to represent them and negotiate a contract with a team

35. Players' organizations have done much to change the legal status of athletes in various professional sports. However, it is often difficult to get players to join any organization that may ask them to participate in a strike. This is because athletes
   a.   come from very conservative family backgrounds
   b.   see themselves more as spectators than as workers
   c.   have such short playing careers and are partly dependent on owners*
   d.   have such strong team spirit and loyalty to the team owners who originally gave them a contract

36. The legal status of professional athletes in individual sports depends on the rules of professional organizations and
   a.   special rights guaranteed by local government agencies
   b.   contractual agreements made with sponsors, agents, and managers*
   c.   the age, race, and gender of the athlete
   d.   the ethical principles of people in the sport being played

37. According to data presented in the chapter, professional athletes playing for minor league sport teams
   a.   usually make less than $3500 per month*
   b.   make about half of the average salaries in the top professional leagues
   c.   make nearly the same as athletes in the top professional leagues
   d.   make less than minimum wage in the U.S. and Canada

37. The salaries of professional athletes in team sports in the U.S.
   a.   are highest in the sports involving the most danger and risk
   b.   have always been higher than the average incomes of top corporate executives
   c.   tend to go down when team owners must compete with one another to sign players to contracts
   d.   reflect the legal status of players plus the revenues generated by those sports*

38. The recent, large annual increases in the salaries of athletes in the major men's professional sport leagues were primarily due to
   a.   increased gate receipts in major league baseball
   b.   a change in the legal status of players and the increased popularity of sports as entertainment*
   c.   a switch from family ownership of teams to corporate ownership of teams
   d.   the development of cable television coverage

39. The large annual increases in the salaries of major league baseball players after the 1976 season were due in large part to
    a.   increases in the popularity of baseball outside North America
    b.   a change in the legal status of players*
    c.   a switch from family ownership of teams to corporate ownership of teams
    d.   the development of cable television coverage

40. If you were the head of the Major League Players' Association and you wanted to get support from fans as you negotiated a new contract with baseball owners, which salary figure would be most likely to turn off fan support?
    a.   the median salary of players
    b.   the modal salary of players
    c.   the mean salary of players*
    d.   the minimum salary of players

41. According to the author, many of the professional athletes in individual sports make
    a.   more money than many people think because they get a guaranteed share of all gate receipts
    b.   less money than many people think because they must pay for officials and promotional expenses
    c.   less money than many people think because they pay their own expenses*
    d.   more money than many people think because they all have private sponsors

42. Large salaries for professional athletes in U.S. team sports may often serve the interests of team owners because
    a.   large salaries create team loyalty among players
    b.   large salaries attract spectators and media coverage*
    c.   highly paid teams are usually winning teams
    d.   highly paid athletes are much easier to control

43. The author argues that the incomes of professional athletes are generally justified in economic terms, but they raise questions about
    a.   educational systems, especially in North America
    b.   the meanings of work and leisure
    c.   the values and priorities in our culture*
    d.   the business training received by aspiring young athletes

44. The author explains that the endorsement incomes of athletes in the U.S. indicate that race and gender are
    a.   important factors influencing a person's advertising value*
    b.   in no way connected to a person's advertising value
    c.   less important than age in determining advertising value
    d.   only important in the southern states of the U.S.

45.   Research reviewed in the chapter shows that ticket prices to sport events are primarily a function of
   a.   the salaries and prize winnings of athletes
   b.   the amount of media coverage attracted by the event
   c.   the average incomes of spectators in the area
   d.   the spectator demand for tickets*

46.   The author notes that the legal status of amateur athletes around the world are controlled by
   a.   various organizations, each with their own interests and goals*
   b.   a single international commission on amateur sports
   c.   the parents of the athletes
   d.   various player organizations in different sports

47.   In his discussion of the legal status of amateur athletes in U.S. intercollegiate sports, the author suggests that there is a need for
   a.   clinical studies of how athletes cope with having few rights
   b.   sport agents in every university
   c.   individuals and groups charged with advocating the interests of athletes*
   d.   required college courses on the economics of sports

ESSAY QUESTIONS

1.   Commercial sports prosper in certain types of societies. Using the U.S., Canada, England, or Australia as an example, explain how the characteristics of any one of those countries provide a strong supports for maintaining commercial sports.

2.   The sports editor of your local newspaper writes an editorial in which he claims that popular commercial sports such as NFL football are wonderful because they have nothing to do with class relations and class differences between people. In fact, he says that they promote the overall democratization of society. You want to challenge his conclusion in a letter to the editor. Use the material in this chapter to write your critical letter.

3.   Spectator interest in sports varies from one society to another. Some powerful and wealthy people in a country undergoing economic expansion want to create a high level of spectator interest in sports throughout their society. They hire someone to survey the sociology of sport to discover what can be done to create spectator interests. On the basis of material in this chapter, what do you think the consultant will tell them?

4.   You have been asked by a major "think tank" to serve as a consultant on a project that is trying to predict what sports may look like from a global perspective in the year 2010. What would you predict about the globalization of sports over the next decade? Explain the basis for your predictions.

5. Transnational corporations are using sports as vehicles for global expansion to a greater degree than ever before. Why do these large corporations see sports and sport sponsorships as important in their growth? Are they interested only in immediate profits or do they have longer term goals? If so, what are those goals?

6. A "good game" usually refers to one in which uncertainty and "stakes" were high, and good plays were frequent. Choose a sport and show how the basic format and goals, the orientations of participants, and the organizations controlling the sport have been changed to emphasize these three factors.

7. In commercial sports, there is a tendency for heroic values to be emphasized more than aesthetic values. Choose a sport and show how commercialization has effected the values and orientations emphasized by athletes, coaches, media announcers, and spectators.

8. Basketball player Dennis Rodman explains that his value as a pro athlete is related strongly to his flair and style. In what ways is Rodman's statement consistent with the general thesis about the effects of commercialization on sports as explained in the chapter?

9. Some people take the position that commercialization always corrupts sports. After reading about the effects of commercialization in the chapter, would you agree or disagree with such a position? Explain your response.

10. In your business class a student says that if you want to make money, buy a sports team. You join the discussion and say that owning a sport team is not always a good investment. You are asked to explain. How do you respond?

11. In your business class, a student says that NFL football is an inspiration to all who believe that competition is the driving force behind all progress and development in society. The instructor knows you're in this sociology of sport class and asks you to respond to the remark. What would you say? Would you agree or disagree? Explain.

12. Art Model, owner of the Baltimore Ravens of the NFL, once said that the owners of the NFL teams were "28 republicans who vote socialist." What did he mean by this statement?

13. Many cities in North America are subsidizing professional sport team owners to some degree. Cities often provide public funds to build stadiums and arenas. Such support for teams is justified by beliefs that pro teams are good for the economy of a metropolitan area. Do you agree or disagree with this justification?

14. Professional team owners in recent years have made new demands for cities to fund to stadiums and arenas. They say that they cannot make money without the new facilities. Is this true? How do stadiums contribute to revenue streams for team owners?

15. Your campus has just received $30 million from a large soft drink company. In return, the soft drink company can use all sport teams and athletes to promote their products, and no other company's soft drinks can be sold on your campus for the next 10 years. In terms of the goals and organization of amateur sports, what are the pros and cons of such an arrangement?

16. The legal status of professional athletes in U.S. team sports has traditionally been regulated by the "reserve system." Describe the characteristics of the reserve system, and show how those characteristics have had an impact on the salaries earned by professional athletes. What has happened to athletes salaries as various aspects of the reserve system have been eliminated?

17. Choose two professional sports - one team sport and one individual sport - and compare the legal status of the athletes in each. If you were an athlete which situation would you prefer?

18. A friend of yours has two sons and a daughter. He is encouraging each of them to develop their sport skills so they can become pro athletes. He tells you that "professional athletes have it made financially." How would you respond to your friend?

19. You and some friends are on your way to a rock concert for which tickets cost $40.00 per person. As you walk into the stadium, someone says she hasn't been in the stadium very often because the tickets to sport events are so expensive. Another friend notes that tickets are so expensive because of the high salaries paid to pro athletes. He says the athletes are not worth the high salaries they receive and that they often don't need the salaries because they make so much on endorsements. What are the weaknesses in your friend's explanation?

20. Many amateur sports are faced with an interesting paradox: the skills of amateur athletes generate money, but the definition of amateurism maintained by many sport organizations prevents the athletes from sharing in that money. Show how this paradox exists in both intercollegiate sports and international track and field, and make some policy recommendations that would lead to fair and constructive changes.

21. As televised sports become increasingly popular around the world and as athletes become even more visible as international media celebrities, the revenues that come into sport organizations and the salaries paid to athletes will continue to increase. Should there be new rules enabling cities to tax these "windfall" profits and then use the revenue to support youth sports and school sports in the city? Would you vote for such a policy if it were on the ballot? Explain why or why not.

CHAPTER 12
SPORTS AND THE MEDIA:
could they survive without each other?

CHAPTER OUTLINE

I. Unique features of the media

II. Sports and the media: a two-way relationship
   - A. Do sports depend on the media?
     - 1. Have commercial sports sold out to the media?
     - 2. Have the media corrupted sports?
   - B. Do the media depend on sports?
     - 1. Newspapers
     - 2. Television companies
   - C. Sports and the media: a symbiotic relationship fueled by economic forces
   (BOX: "Television and the Olympic Games: a marriage of mutual interest")

III. Images and messages in media sports
   - A. How the media constructs sports
   - B. Themes underlying images and messages
     - 1. Success themes
     - 2. Masculinity and femininity themes
     - 3. Race themes
     - 4. Other ideological themes in mediated sports
   - C. Media impact on sport-related behaviors
     - 1. Active participation in sports
     - 2. Attendance at sports events
     - 3. Gambling on sports
   - D. Audience experiences with media sports

IV. The profession of sports journalism
   - A. Before television: when sports*writers* created the images and messages
   - B. After television: a new age for sports journalists
   - C. Ethics and sports journalism
   - D. Sportswriters and sports announcers: a comparison

V. Conclusion: could sports and the media live without each other?

MULTIPLE CHOICE QUESTIONS

1.   The chapter on sports and the media is based on the assumption that
      a.   human beings around the world are basically slaves to the media
      b.   the power of the media has no limits
      c.   media content informs people's lives and social worlds*
      d.   most people define the media as unimportant in their lives

2.   Which of the following is *not* an accurate statement about sports and the media?
      a.   all media coverage involves selective re-presentations of sports and sport events
      b.   the media offset and generally reverse the effects of commercialization on sports*
      c.   the media open up new opportunities for spectators to have access to sport events
      d.   the media limit and influence our perspectives on the sports they present to us

3.   According to the author, the media are generally organized to serve three major functions in a society. Which of the following is *not* one of those functions?
      a.   to provide entertainment in a variety of forms
      b.   to provide interpretations of what is happening in the world
      c.   to provide information about events and other people
      d.   to provide images that blur the distinction between reality and fantasy*

4.   In countries where the media are privately owned, their major interest is profit making; and in countries where the media are controlled and operated by the state, the major interest is
      a.   shaping values and providing a public service*
      b.   generating revenues for the state
      c.   funding artists who work for the state
      d.   creating images that expand people's experiences

5.   According to the author, those people who make media content decisions as they select the images and messages to be re-presented through the media are best described as
      a.   image and message "filters"*
      b.   propaganda artists
      c.   agents of corporate capitalism
      d.   political prophets

6.   The author notes that the media and media content are tied to power relations primarily in the sense that they
     a.   cause people to raise questions about major political and economic decisions in society
     b.   usually give priority to images and messages consistent with dominant ideologies in a society*
     c.   are direct reflections of the interests of people in positions of political power
     d.   are controlled and censored by the most powerful people in the society

7.   When the media are privately owned, a televised sport event is "re-produced" in a way that usually emphasizes
     a.   the dramatic content of the event*
     b.   a critical perspective on sports and sport participants
     c.   how much work goes into preparing for a sport event
     d.   the specific technical skills of athletes

8.   According to the author, what we see and hear in a televised presentation of a sport event is
     a.   a set of images and descriptions that accurately summarize the content of the event itself
     b.   an artificial set of images and messages designed to deceive viewers for the purpose of entertainment
     c.   a visual summary of all the action and a description of what really underlies the action
     d.   a carefully edited and selective version of images and messages*

9.   In the discussion of the relationship between sports and the media in the U.S., it was pointed out that
     a.   commercial sports depend on the media, but the media do not depend on sports
     b.   the media depend on sports but sports do not depend on the media
     c.   both the media and commercial sports have grown to depend on each other for commercial success*
     d.   even though they are connected to each other, neither sports nor the media really depend on each other

10. According to Leonard Koppett, sports are unique forms of entertainment because
     a.   after they finish, many people are interested in discussing them further*
     b.   they are one of the few forms of entertainment having no real production costs
     c.   other entertainment events do not receive the same publicity as sport events
     d.   sports appeal mainly to the intellectual interests of those who watch them

11. Sport organizations and sport sponsors often try to make money from "rights fees." These fees consist of money paid
    a. by media organizations to re-present particular events for their own purposes*
    b. by spectators who then have the right to watch events
    c. by lawyers who then have the right to legally advise all those involved in the production of an event
    d. by journalists who write about an event for newspapers or magazines

12. Because of the size of television audiences and the deregulation of the television industry, television rights fees have increased dramatically. According to the author, this increase has
    a. led to limits on athletes' salaries
    b. increased the profitability of commercial sports*
    c. enabled public organizations to sponsor more sports
    d. destroyed the profitability of commercial sports

13. Have sports sold out to the media? According to the author, the most accurate answer to this question is that those who control sports
    a. have tried to produce a generally marketable entertainment package for spectators and sponsors*
    b. do not understand the power of the media
    c. have become slaves to the media
    d. are so eager to please the media that they make changes for nothing in return

14. The people who try to make the case that television has corrupted sports generally overlook two major points: (1) television people are not the only people who make decisions about sports, and (2)
    a. television people realize that no matter what they do, some people will always watch their programs
    b. the people most directly connected with sports are usually unconcerned about television coverage
    c. television itself is influenced and regulated by the political and economic context in which it operates*
    d. changes in sports generally reflect the interests of athletes over and above anything else

15. According to the author, the media most dependent on sports are
    a. books and magazines
    b. the Internet and radio
    c. newspapers and television*
    d. television and film

16. If other major city newspapers were like *The Chicago Tribune*, we could conclude that since the turn of the century, the proportion of their newsprint devoted to sports has
    a. increased at a steady rate*
    b. stayed about the same except for a slight increase during the 1950s
    c. declined steadily except during the war years
    d. gone up and down with the popularity of high school sports

17. According to estimates given by people who study the media, what percentage of the overall circulation of major city newspapers is tied to the existence of the sports section?
    a. less than 10%
    b. between 10% and 20%
    c. about 30%*
    d. about 50%

18. The author explains that even though many sport events often receive low ratings, American television companies are interested in broadcasting them because they fill "dead time" on weekends and because they
    a. last longer than a normal half-hour or one-hour show
    b. bring family members together around the television
    c. appeal to children and other impressionable people
    d. attract a special, hard-to-reach audience*

19. Golf and tennis are two of the more frequently covered sports on television. The reason for this is that they
    a. have more viewers than most other sport events
    b. are tied to the real estate and corporate interests of television executives
    c. attract advertising revenues from companies that want to reach high-income consumers*
    d. have a special character that attracts people interested in pure sports

20. According to the data presented in Table 12-2, the rights fees for major sport events have
    a. gone up and down with major economic trends
    b. increased steadily*
    c. declined steadily
    d. remained stable over the past 20 years

21. The author suggests that pay-per-view (PPV) sports programming will
    a. increase in the future*
    b. disappear in the future
    c. destroy special interest sports such as boxing
    d. limit the profitability of commercial sports

22.   Rupert Murdoch, who owns major television companies around the world, has used sport programming to
       a.   develop friendly relationships with other television companies
       b.   fuel a global corporate media expansion strategy*
       c.   generate financial losses he can used as tax deductions
       d.   establish relationships with high profile athletes around the world

23.   In the special boxed discussion of the relationship between television and the Olympic Games it was concluded that
       a.   network television has stopped paying large amounts of money to broadcast the Olympic Games
       b.   television companies have dictated significant changes in the basic goals and format of Olympic events
       c.   television rights fees have created windfall revenues for the IOC enabling it to become more powerful*
       d.   the balance of power in the relationship is clearly on the side of the Olympics

24.   According to the author what one word best summarizes the relationship between sports and the media?
       a.   manipulative
       b.   dead-end
       c.   changing
       d.   symbiotic*

25.   The author explains that global corporations have become increasingly involved as sponsors of sports for many reasons. Which of the following is *not* one of those reasons discussed by the author?
       a.   sport events attract worldwide attention among potential consumers of corporate products
       b.   sport images and athletes can be used to market products worldwide
       c.   sports are politically charged events that can attract or repel consumers*
       d.   sport images can be used to promote a way of life based on consumption and competition

26.   Corporations that profit from alcohol or tobacco sales have often sponsored sports because
       a.   athletes are notorious abusers of both products
       b.   research shows that both substances help athletes control anxiety during sport participation
       c.   their executives have higher sport participation rates than executives in other corporations
       d.   it enables them to associate their products with an activity that most people define as healthy*

27. The author points out that, just like Hollywood films and television soap operas, mediated sports (that is, those we see on television) are
   a. violence producers
   b. symbolic constructions*
   c. male identity rituals
   d. anti-social influences in society

28. Research on the media suggests that the images and messages associated with televised sports in the U.S. tend to emphasize, among other things,
   a. competition and the emotions and personalities of athletes*
   b. teamwork and coach-athlete relationships
   c. the connection between fans in the stands and the athletes on the field
   d. the friendships between those who compete against each other in sports

29. There are major differences between the sports coverage presented in the print media and coverage presented in the broadcast media (see table). Which of the following accurately describes one of these differences?
   a. print media emphasize action while broadcast media emphasize analysis
   b. the success of print media depends more on credibility while the success of broadcast media depends more on hype*
   c. the content of print media provides more uncritical support for sports and sport personalities than does the content of broadcast media
   d. the coverage of print media is focused while the coverage of the broadcast media is diversified

30. Which of the following is *not* characteristic of the coverage of sport by the broadcast media? They tend to
   a. emphasize elite sport competition
   b. emphasize outcomes at the expense of the process of participation
   c. be concerned with the private lives of sport personalities
   d. present games in ways that destroy spectator awareness of action.*

31. When Lever and Wheeler studied how *The Chicago Tribune* covered sports between 1900 and 1975, they found that over the years an increasing amount of coverage was devoted to
   a. local high school sports
   b. violent and aggressive sports
   c. elite, professional sports*
   d. sports played by local people in Chicago

32. In Joan Chandler's comparison of media broadcasts of sport events in the U.S. and England, she found that British broadcasters were more likely than their American counterparts to
   a. focus on final scores
   b. emphasize the role of women in sports
   c. discuss the element of risk in sports
   d. downplay the importance of competition*

33. Research on the media coverage of men's and women's sports has generally found that coverage
    a. emphasizes women's sports involving strength and power more than sports emphasizing grace and beauty
    b. of men and women has become almost equal over the past 10 years, with about 40% going to women's events on a worldwide basis
    c. of women's sports contains confused messages about strength and weakness and about power and appearance*
    d. presents women's events as having special importance and significance while men's events are presented in a matter-of-fact manner

34. If you were reading a story about a women's sport event in a North American newspaper or magazine, you would expect which of the following?
    a. the headline for the story would be in larger type than other headlines and it would probably be on Page One
    b. there would be more photos with the story than with sports stories about men
    c. the photos run with the story would be less likely to show sports action than photos in stories about men*
    d. the story would be written by a woman journalist and appear in a regular feature section on women's sports

35. According to the research review in the chapter, the media coverage of women's sports tends to
    a. focus on sport activities that fit traditional images of women*
    b. emphasize activities in which women display speed and strength
    c. promote events which people do not care about
    d. accurately reflect the changing roles of women in today's societies

36. After reading the review of differential coverage given to men's and women's sports, it could be concluded that at least part of the difference in newspaper coverage has been due to the
    a. work routines of sportswriters and the formats of sports sections in papers*
    b. inability of women sportswriters to cover events in the same ways that men cover them
    c. lack of exciting action in competition between women athletes
    d. problems that women coaches and athletes have when they deal with the press

37. Research suggests that people in the media have made serious attempts to avoid stereotypes in their coverage. The author suggests that one way to reduce all forms of racial bias in the media is to
    a. give more coverage to white athletes
    b. avoid all comments about the physical abilities of black athletes
    c. hire more ethnic minorities in all media jobs*
    d. stress the importance of sports in the lives of minorities

38. Studies using critical theory as a guide have identified a number of themes in the images and messages of mediated sports in the U.S. Which of the following is *not* one of the themes that has been identified?
    a. mental and physical aggression
    b. nationalism and national unity
    c. cooperation and social solidarity*
    d. consumerism

39. The theme of teamwork emphasized in the images and messages in mediated sports in the U.S. often promotes
    a. loyalty and productivity in organizational terms*
    b. cooperation for the sake of personal satisfaction
    c. achievement based on respect and awareness of the needs of others
    d. achieving personal goals by helping others achieve their goals

40. Which of the following fits with the author's conclusions about how the behavior of spectators is influenced by consuming media re-presentations of sports?
    a. if media did not cover sports, gambling on sports would not exist
    b. people who watch sports on television have higher rates of obesity than others from similar backgrounds
    c. the media have a positive effect on attendance at sport events at all levels of competition
    d. as a group, people who consume media sports are no more or less likely to be active in sports themselves*

41. Research on the role of watching televised sports among married couples in the U.S. has found that
    a. watching sports is more positive than disruptive for most married couples*
    b. watching televised sports is the number one leisure activity for most married couples
    c. over half of all married women can be classified as "football widows"
    d. married couples argue more about what sports they watch than they argue over any other type of programming

42. The author notes that sportswriters who worked before the days of television were more likely than the sportswriters of today to
    a. use their words to create heroes*
    b. try to uncover weaknesses among athletes
    c. discuss conflicts between players and coaches
    d. be critical of team strategies and tactics

43. The author argues that since television began to cover sports, the relationship between athletes and sportswriters has
    a. improved dramatically
    b. become characterized by strain and tension*
    c. been characterized by mutual identification
    d. become better than relationships between TV announcers and athletes

44.	According to Leonard Koppett one of the major factors which continues to interfere with the objectivity of sports reporters is that they
    a.	tend to take on the attitudes of the people they cover when they get to know those people*
    b.	are usually on the payrolls of teams and team owners
    c.	are frequently "bought off" with favors and cash by people with special interests
    d.	usually develop strong anti-sport attitudes after five to seven years

45.	According to the discussion in the chapter, which of the following accurately describes differences between the role of sportswriter and the role of sports announcer?
    a.	sportswriters have higher levels of public recognition than announcers have
    b.	sportswriters have fewer opportunities to do investigative reporting than announcers have
    c.	sportswriters have more job security than announcers have*
    d.	sportswriters have less freedom of expression than announcers have

46.	When the author refers to "vidiated sports" in his conclusion to the chapter, he is referring to sports that are
    a.	re-presented to audiences in entertaining forms through video technology*
    b.	recently televised in forms that involve the use of virtual reality
    c.	made just for television sports such as "The Gladiators" and similar programs
    d.	played through video game technology either at home or in video arcades

---

ESSAY QUESTIONS

1.	One of the paradoxes associated with the media coverage of sports is that the media open up new opportunities for spectators to view sports, but they also limit and define the experiences of spectators. Explain how the media can do both these things simultaneously.

2.	Experiencing a sport event through the media is different than experiencing the same event in person. Pick a sport that you have attended in person and also watched on television, and explain the major differences between the two experiences. What are the origins of those differences? In your explanation, discuss the notion that a televised sport is a "re-presented" version of the event.

3.	We have all played sports that do not depend on the media. But commercial sports are different than recreational sports, and they depend on the media for their success. Explain the differences between recreational and commercial sports in a way that indicates how and why commercial sports depend on the media.

4.   One of your anti-television friends says that television has corrupted sports in your country. A discussion begins when you raise questions about her conclusion. She says that sports have changed considerably over the past 20 years, and the changes have gone hand-in-hand with the growth of television coverage. You say that just because two things happen at the same time does not mean that one is causing the other. She wants you to explain your point in more detail. Use material from the chapter to build your case.

5.   People often forget that the media depends on sports as much as sports depends on the media. Illustrate this point by describing what might have happened to newspapers and/or television over the past 40 years if sports had never been included in newspaper sports sections or TV programming. What would newspapers and/or television be like today without sports coverage or programming?

6.   What if television did not exist? Describe what commercial sports would be like today if there had never been television coverage of sports over the past 45 years. Use examples from sports at all levels of organization (high school, college, amateur, and professional) as you create your description. Would the sports themselves be different? Would the spectator experience be different?

7.   A few television companies around the world have paid massive amounts of money for the rights to cover certain sport events, even when they don't anticipate that the ratings will be as high as they are for prime time programming. Why would television companies be so eager to cover sports in light of the fact that they seldom attract massive audiences, except in the case of a limited number of special events?

8.   In 1972, the U.S. television rights to the Munich Games sold for about $18 million. In 1996, 24 years later, the IOC sold the U.S. rights to the Olympic Games in 2000, 2002, 2004, 2006, and 2008 for $3.6 billion; the Japanese rights for the same games were sold for $545.5 million; and the European and Asian rights were also sold for large amounts of money. Why have the rights for the Olympic Games increased so dramatically? Has the IOC prostituted the games in order to make quick profits for itself and its members? Or has the IOC used the media to promote its own goals?

9.   People without detailed knowledge about a particular sport often say they would rather watch the sport on TV than read about it in the newspaper. Why is this? What are the major differences between the ways sports are covered in the print media versus the ways they are covered in the broadcast media?

10.   The author makes the point that mediated sports are symbolic constructions, just as Hollywood films and television soap operas are symbolic constructions. What is meant by this point, and what is involved in the media construction of sports?

11. The images and messages underlying media coverage of sports in the United States often revolve around success, masculinity and femininity, and race. What are some of the major themes emphasized in these images and messages? Do you think these themes have an impact on the way you or others think about or explain how the social world around you operates or how it should operate?

12. Reviews of the images and messages of mediated sports in the U.S. have identified ideological themes such as nationalism and national unity, individual efforts to achieve victory, teamwork, mental and physical aggression, and consumerism. Would these same ideological themes be emphasized in the images and messages presented in mediated sports in all countries? Why or why not? Give some examples of what you might expect to be emphasized in other cultures.

13. The author states that the coverage of sports in North American media has probably had a major impact on how people in Canada and the U.S. think about masculinity, femininity, and gender relations as a whole. Use material from the chapter and from your personal experience to either agree or disagree with this statement.

14. You're a new editor at *Sports Illustrated*. At your first editorial meeting the major item on the agenda is a debate about the February swimsuit issue. As the discussion goes on, it is decided that it would be economically unwise to drop the swimsuit issue. But it is also decided that if the swimsuit issue is continued, there must be other changes in the magazine to present a fair image of women in sports. As a new editor, you are called on to make some suggestions for changes. How would you respond?

15. The next item on the agenda at the *Sports Illustrated* editor's meeting is a motion to publish a full set of betting lines for every major sport event scheduled for the upcoming week. After a short discussion, the question is called and you are asked to vote on the motion. Would you support it or not? Why?

16. You are called in as an advisor to the President's Council on Fitness and Sports. The two topics being discussed are (1) whether television sports are turning people in the U.S. into couch potatoes, and (2) whether the television coverage of professional sports is destroying people's interests in local high school, college, and amateur sports. The Council wants advice from you. What do you tell them?

17. Imagine yourself as a 75-year-old sportswriter with over 50 years experience in the field. Write a short autobiography in which you describe what sportswriting was like before television started covering sports and how it has changed since television entered the scene. Indicate whether you are happy you worked when you did or whether you wish you were just starting out now.

18.   One of the students in your sport sociology course catches your instructor off guard with a question about the differences between a sport sociologist and a sport reporter from a newspaper like *The Chicago Tribune*. You know that your chances for a good grade will be improved if you can come to the instructor's rescue with an explanation of your own. What would you say in answer to the question?

19.   Video games are becoming increasingly sophisticated in terms of their ability to simulate the athletes and actions of television sports. Do you think that video game sports will ever become as popular as televised sports? Explain why or why not. In your explanation emphasize the differences between the two experiences.

CHAPTER 13
SPORTS, POLITICS, AND THE STATE:
what makes sports political?

CHAPTER OUTLINE

I.   The sports - government connection
    A.   Safeguarding the public order
    B.   Maintaining and developing fitness and physical abilities
    C.   Promoting the prestige of a group, community, or nation
    D.   Promoting a sense of identity, belonging, and unity
    (BOX: "Unity for What? The political consequences of cheering for the home team")
    E.   Emphasizing values and orientations consistent with dominant political ideology
    F.   Increasing citizen support for individual political leaders and government itself
    G.   To promote general economic development in the community of society

II.   Sports and global political processes
    A.   International sports: ideals versus realities
        1.   Nation-states, sports, and cultural ideology
    B.   New political realities in an era of transnational corporations
    C.   Other global political issues
        1.   Athletes as global migrant workers
        2.   Global politics and the production of sport equipment and clothing
    D.   Making sense of new political realities
    (BOX: "The Olympic Games: what makes them special?)

III. Politics in sports
    A.   What qualifies as a sport?
    B.   What are the rules of a sport?
    C.   Who makes and enforces rules in sports?
    D.   Who organizes and controls games, meets, matches and tournaments?
    E.   Where will sport events take place?
    F.   Who is eligible to participate in a sport?
    G.   How will rewards be distributed to athletes and other organizational members?

IV.   Conclusion: what makes sports political?

MULTIPLE CHOICE QUESTIONS

1. In the chapter introduction, the author notes that the study of politics today
    a. is limited to analyzing the policies and regulations of nation-states
    b. has ignored political relationships between capitalist nations
    c. covers so many topics and issues that it has become meaningless in the real world
    d. has been extended to cover many forms of power, including the ability to influence ideas and values*

2. In the chapter introduction, the author makes a distinction between power and authority. Power refers to the ability to influence, and authority refers to
    a. all formal positions held by members of organizations
    b. a form of power that comes with a recognized and legitimate position in an organization or set of relationships*
    c. any person who has been able to gain control over others for the purpose of serving the common good
    d. any form of power enabling a person to influence others, even against their will.

3. As sports become increasingly complex in societies, government involvement tends to increase because governments are often the only organizations with
    a. the cash needed to pay high salaries to athletes
    b. the power and capital needed to sponsor events and construct major facilities*
    c. officials who do not have conflicts of interests that might interfere with developing connections with sports
    d. the legal connections needed to deal with nationwide groups connected with sports leagues

4. When governmental organizations regulate access to sport facilities and make rules about who can engage in what sports activities under what circumstances, the major stated reason for their intervention into sports is to
    a. improve fitness and health among disadvantaged people
    b. increase the legitimacy of their control over people
    c. safeguard the public order*
    d. promote community integration and solidarity

5. After reading the chapter, it could be concluded that government involvement in promoting fitness among the general population is most likely in countries where
    a. people are covered by private medical insurance instead of national health insurance
    b. there are high proportions of fast food restaurants
    c. worker alienation is relatively high
    d. there are national health insurance and socialized medicine programs*

6. Many people believe that participation in organized, competitive sports improves fitness and health, and therefore lowers health care costs. This belief is
   a. consistently supported by data from college and pro sports in the U.S.
   b. promoted by people who have an interest in turning socialist countries into capitalist countries
   c. often contradicted by information about what actually happens in connection with sport participation*
   d. valid only in capitalist countries where sports are highly competitive

7. The government of the former Soviet Union promoted citizen involvement in "physical culture" because Soviet officials generally believed that physical fitness was connected to
   a. a spiritual commitment to communism
   b. an attractive physical appearance that would impress people from other countries
   c. a decrease in family size and willingness to care for older relatives
   d. lower rates of worker absenteeism and higher rates of worker productivity*

8. An increasing number of governments have policies for paying cash rewards to their citizens who win medals as athletes in major international competitions. According to the author, this practice is based primarily on the idea that
   a. athletes need money and other material support to be competitive with people from other countries
   b. success by individuals in sports brings prestige as well as other benefits to the country as a whole*
   c. athletes who get paid for winning medals will become more patriotic and supportive of the government
   d. every medal won by a country's athletes increases the per capita income in that country

9. In many cases, sports do bring people together and create "emotional unity" within a population. But the author argues that a sociological understanding of the significance of this unity requires that we ask questions about
   a. the characteristics of the athletes who create this unity
   b. how the unity affects the performance of sport teams
   c. the social and political consequences of the unity*
   d. the different types of unity and identity created by different sports

10. In the discussion of sports and social identity, belonging, and unity, the author explains that sports
   a. have special qualities that make them especially powerful mechanisms of social change in society
   b. provide models of what all forms of social organization should be like
   c. produce forms of social unity that cannot be produced by other activities
   d. do little to alter the realities of life among people, especially powerless people, in a country*

144

11. The author explains that if sports in a particular country have an effect on the political values and orientations of people in that country, it probably occurs in connection with
   a. the vocabulary and stories that accompany sports*
   b. the actual success of national sport teams
   c. the political attitudes of athletes and coaches
   d. the degree to which sports are funded by public money

12. When Germany hosted the 1936 Olympic Games in Berlin, Hitler used the Olympics Games to
   a. discover and recruit officers for the German army
   b. promote the Nazi ideology of "Nordic supremacy"*
   c. test Jews and gentiles in competitive events
   d. isolate the German people from the rest of the world

13. According to the conclusions of political scientists, the practice of using sports to generate political support occurs in connection with what type of governments?
   a. autocratic governments, but not democratic governments
   b. democratic governments, but not autocratic governments
   c. all governments*
   d. governments in industrial societies only

14. The author explains that when governments sponsor sports and political officials affiliate themselves with sports, their primary purpose is often to
   a. increase their power in international politics
   b. increase their legitimacy in the eyes of citizens*
   c. show voters that sports are connected with politics
   d. gain political credibility in the eyes of political scientists

15. The author argues that government involvement in sports is usually connected in some way with
   a. the sport experiences of political officials
   b. power struggles between groups in a society or community*
   c. the need for politicians to appear physically fit in the eyes of voters
   d. the unique interests of poor and powerless people in a society or community

16. The author notes that government officials are most likely to use sports as a diplomatic tool when
   a. vital national interests are at stake
   b. officials are negotiating crucial national and international policies
   c. there is a need for cultural exchanges and general communication between officials from different countries*
   d. national teams have just been victorious in major international competitions

17. When the author reviews information on the connection between sports and international relations, he suggests that sports
    a. shape how vital national interests are negotiated in international politics
    b. are most often used as forms of public diplomacy*
    c. only influence political relationships between powerful countries such as the U. S. and China
    d. are unrelated to all aspects of international relations

18. The history of sports, especially the Olympic Games, has shown that for most nations the real primary purpose underlying participation in international sport events has been to
    a. promote international understanding
    b. control the lives of citizens in repressive ways
    c. pursue national political interests*
    d. create new political leaders

19. The author suggests that international sport events are covered differently by U.S. television companies now that the Cold War has ended. According to the author, current coverage is
    a. less likely to emphasize nationalist themes*
    b. more likely to emphasize a nation versus nation theme
    c. more likely to emphasize extreme forms of patriotism
    d. likely to ignore the national affiliation of all athletes

20. In the discussion of sports and cultural ideology, the author notes that one of the problems associated with using sports to bridge diplomatic and cultural gaps between peoples of the world is that sports may
    a. unfairly force economically powerful nations to contribute to the economies of less powerful countries
    b. promote ideologies and consumption patterns that lead powerless nations to become more dependent on powerful nations*
    c. enable powerless nations to take unfair advantage of people and resources in powerful nations
    d. lead to worldwide migration patterns that upset the sex ratios of powerful and less powerful nations

21. According to the author, it is rare for sports to be vehicles for meaningful cultural exchanges between countries. Meaningful cultural exchanges are most likely to occur when
    a. there is a mutual sharing of information and an increase in self-sufficiency among developing nations*
    b. athletes from developing nations get the training they need to win medals in international competitions
    c. the sports produce "cultural converts" to the lifestyles of economically powerful nations
    d. nations with traditional cultures abandon their folk games and play sports from powerful industrialized nations

146

22. Global politics have changed dramatically since the mid-1980s. According to the author's analysis, these changes have made international sports
    a.   less important than in the past when the Cold War influenced international politics
    b.   more important as political events than as commercial events
    c.   important stages for commercial displays by large, transnational corporations*
    d.   less profitable for all sponsors, including corporate sponsors

23. The author argues that in recent years, sports have become framed in new political terms. Which of the following best describes these terms?
    a.   product logo identification has become as important as national identification*
    b.   national loyalties and national identities are no longer important
    c.   events are now athletic-political rather than athletic-economic
    d.   events are now shown as "free market economies vs. planned economies"

24. Large multinational corporations are becoming more frequent sponsors of sports around the world. According to the author, corporate sponsorships are primarily motivated by an interest in
    a.   promoting a way of life based on consumption and consumerism*
    b.   developing a single worldwide standard of living
    c.   findings new ways to train workers who will produce their goods
    d.   building sports that bring the world together in large competitive events

25. The author argues that to the extent that the media coverage of international sports is sponsored by corporations, international events become vehicles for presenting messages
    a.   to spectator-citizens
    b.   on behalf of environmental groups
    c.   in the interest of world-wide socialism
    d.   to spectator-consumers*

26. According to the author's analysis, the images and messages presented by the sponsors of major sport events tend to
    a.   dictate what people think
    b.   influence what people think about*
    c.   be ignored by nearly all spectators
    d.   discourage most people from a way of life based on consumption

27. In the boxed section on the Olympic Games, the author argues that the planning, promoting, presenting, and playing of the Olympics is now designed primarily to
    a.   promote international peace and understanding
    b.   help people to understand and appreciate differences among cultures and human beings
    c.   help people in the television audience visualize forms of global community
    d.   promote the commercial interests of corporate sponsors*

28. Bruce Kidd, a former Olympian and now a physical educator, has suggested that the Olympics be changed so that
    a.   the personal tragedies and experiences of athletes can be highlighted in television coverage
    b.   athletes are selected to participate in the games on the basis of their athletic skills only
    c.   the social service and social responsibility of athletes is highlighted in athlete selection and media coverage*
    d.   the needs of corporate sponsors are presented in more human terms

29. When discussing Olympic reforms (in the boxed section), the author suggests a series of changes in the way the Games are planned, promoted, presented, and played. Which of the following is *not* one of those recommended changes?
    a.   limit the number of sports played in wealthy nations with consumption-driven lifestyles
    b.   do away with national uniforms
    c.   eliminate the closing ceremonies*
    d.   eliminate or revise team sports

30. The author's suggestions for reforming the Olympic Games emphasize
    a.   selecting a permanent site for the Olympic Games in a country that has no political interests in sports
    b.   eliminating all medals and individual awards during the Olympics
    c.   promoting the Olympics as "wars without weapons"
    d.   revising the opening ceremonies and eliminating national flags during award ceremonies*

31. The author endorses the elimination of medal counts associated with countries because such counts tend to
    a.   encourage large nations to boycott the Olympics
    b.   defuse nationalism and emphasize fairness
    c.   intensify chauvinism and political differences between countries*
    d.   focus too much on the achievements of individual athletes

32. According to the author, the major advantage for using multiple sites for each Olympic Games would be to
    a.   increase the value of stocks for major world-wide airlines
    b.   discourage wealthy nations from submitting bids to host the Games
    c.   enable corporate sponsors to influence more people around the world
    d.   make it possible for poorer nations to be hosts for the Olympics*

33. According to the author, the Olympic motto of "Citius, Altius, Fortius" should be replaced with new motto that emphasizes
    a.   a spirit of patriotism and nationalism
    b.   the interests of all humanity*
    c.   the evils of corporate capitalism
    d.   the interests of the best athletes in the world

34. The author notes that as sports have become globalized, an increased number of athletes have become global migrant workers. Athletic talent migration raises a number of issues. Which of the following is *not* one of the migration issues discussed in the chapter?
   a.   patterns of personal adjustments among migrating athletes
   b.   the academic success of athletes' children*
   c.   the impact of athlete migration on national identity formation
   d.   the rights of athletes as workers

35. The author notes that the production of sport equipment and clothing is tied to global political processes. In the discussion of this issue, the author points out that the companies producing these goods have
   a.   located production facilities in nations where labor is cheap and labor regulations are scarce*
   a.   avoided locating production facilities outside of industrialized countries
   b.   paid all their workers so much that it has disrupted the economies of poor countries
   c.   formulated a code of ethics that discourages the use of child labor

36. At this point in time, there has not been much research to help us understand the implication of global political processes. The author suggests that to make sense of new political realities
   a.   researchers must assume that sports are becoming modernized and Americanized
   b.   global processes should be ignored so that studies can be done on the local level
   c.   there is a need for research that studies changes on both the global and local levels*
   d.   researchers should focus their attention only on sport forms whose existence can be traced back at least 100 years

37. The author makes the case that politics are an inherent part of sports and sport organizations. Which of the following is *not* one of the aspects of sports that the author describes as involving political processes?
   a.   deciding where sport events will take place
   b.   making and enforcing rules governing competition
   c.   setting goals and motivating athletes, coaches, and sport administrators*
   d.   determining who is eligible to participate in certain sports

38. According to the author, political processes are involved in determining what physical activities qualify as sports in a particular context. The methods used by the IOC to determine what activities will count as sports in the Olympics
   a.   tend to favor the interests of traditional cultures with unique folk games
   b.   have led to increased diversity in culture of sports around the world
   c.   are exactly the same for men's sports as for women's sports
   d.   tend to favor those nations that historically have had the resources to export their games around the world*

39. According to the author, the distribution of rewards in sports involves political processes
    a.   only when it occurs in countries where there are market economies
    b.   in all organized, competitive sports, both amateur and professional*
    c.   in professional sports, but not in amateur sports
    d.   in Western cultures, but not in Eastern cultures

40. After reading the material in the chapter, it could be concluded that
    a.   sports and politics cannot be kept separate*
    b.   sports and politics must be kept separate
    c.   international sports should be abolished because of politics
    d.   officials in one country should regulate *all* international sports so that politics can be controlled

---

ESSAY QUESTIONS

1.   One of your friends is a distance runner who has just made the Olympic track team in your country. He tells you that he doesn't understand why governments have become so involved in sports. You tell him there are a number of reasons why this has happened. He wants you to elaborate. What would you say?

2.   Government involvement in sports occurs on the local level as well as the national level. Using your own community as an example, explain the ways in which sports in your area is touched in some way by government involvement.

3.   You are an assistant personnel director for a very large corporation that insures its own employees. In an effort to reduce health care claims, your boss has suggested the development of a company-wide competitive sports program to get people "in shape." She says that such a program will ultimately cut health care costs. She wants you to critique her ideas. What would you write in your report?

4.   You are a member of the mayor's staff in a large Brazilian city. The staff is debating the possibility of using city funds to subsidize a top-level soccer team. One of the staff members argues that the soccer team can be used to bring city residents together despite their differences, and to create emotional unity within the city. As a representative of a group that is against using city funds in this way, what would you say to counter the argument of this staff member?

5.   In a political science course, one of the students mentions she doesn't understand why American presidents (or Prime Ministers) have traditionally associated themselves with sports. You say that all governments and many government officials use sports to generate political support. How do you back up your statement?

6. Government intervention in sports often impacts the way sports are defined and organized in a community or society. If all the sports programs in your country were sponsored by government organizations, what would they be likely to emphasize?

7. Patterns of sports sponsorship influence the ways sports are organized, promoted, and played. Typically, sports are sponsored by some form of public, government-funded organization or private, corporate-sponsored organization. What might be the major characteristics of sport programs in your community if all sports were sponsored by corporations? What if all sports were sponsored by government organizations? Would there be differences? Explain why or why not.

8. A U.S. official once said, "I think the playing fields of the world will produce the know-how, the democratic exchange, the give-and-take that will open the door to peaceful understanding among all mankind." Give your reasons for either agreeing or disagreeing with this official.

9. The author argues that sports are used often to promote ideas and orientations that fit the interests of the most powerful and wealthy nations in the world. Has this been the case for your country? Explain the ways that your country has used sports to promote its own interests around the world.

10. The author argues that to understand the connection between sports and political processes, it is now necessary to focus on transnational relations as well as international relations. Explain what is meant by transnational relations, and then explain how transnational organizations have joined nation-states in shaping the ways in which sports are defined, organized, planned, promoted, played, and presented around the world.

11. You are on a special committee assigned the task of outlining the goals of the Olympics in the future. Some of the committee members have suggested that the Olympics ought to be abolished because they have become nothing more than marketing sites for powerful transnational corporations. It is up to you to respond to this suggestion. Do you agree or disagree with it? Explain your position in the form of a statement you would make to the entire committee.

12. You have been asked to participate on a special committee to reform the Olympic Games. You are scheduled to make a presentation in which you are to introduce three changes in the way the games are organized. What are the three changes you would suggest and why did you choose them for your presentation?

13. Pick two of the changes recommended by the author when he discusses reforming the Olympic Games and show how and why you think they would not bring about needed reforms. Recommend two alternatives to take their place, and explain why they are better than the ones suggested by the author.

14. You are working in the personnel office of the new Major Soccer League (MSL) in the U.S. It is up to you to make recommendations about the league's policies related to players who are not U.S. citizens. There are two major issues you must deal with: (1) whether there should be limits on the number of non-U.S. citizens on each team, and (2) the support that the league and its teams will provide to athletes coming to the U.S. to play. What would be your recommendations? Explain why you have made them.

15. In a political science class one of your classmates argues that the Olympics are an important force in the arena of international relations. Would you agree or disagree with this student? Give reasons for your position.

16. One of your friends says that powerful countries such as the U.S. and major multinational corporations like Coca Cola are very interested in promoting and even sponsoring international sport events because the events promote their interests. What would you expect your friend to emphasize as he developed is position further?

17. The global expansion of sports and sport organizations has occurred at a very rapid pace over the past decade. Looking at sports from the perspective of a small country with little wealth or power, what are the pros and cons of this expansion?

18. One of your friends gets cut from your high school's softball team. She tells you that the decision to cut her was political, and then she says that politics have no place in sports. You tell her that sports and sport organizations are inherently political. She wants to know how you could even think of making such a comment. What do you say to her?

19. Determining what sports will be included in the Olympics involves political processes. How are new sports included in the Olympics? Does this process favor some nations over others? Explain your answer by using examples of recent sports added to the Olympic list.

20. A friend of yours has lost the use of his legs as a result of a spinal injury sustained in a car accident. He tells you that he is denied the opportunity to participate in varsity sports because of the politics of eligibility that operate in the state high school athletic association. He wants you to join him in making a complaint about the eligibility rules. Would you join him? If so, what would be your argument to the state association? If not, what would you say to your friend?

CHAPTER 14
SPORTS IN HIGH SCHOOL AND COLLEGE:
do varsity sports programs contribute to education?

CHAPTER OUTLINE

I.   Arguments for and against interscholastic sports

II.   Interscholastic sports and the experiences of high school students
        A.   High school student-athletes
        B.   "Student culture" in high schools
                1.   Sports and popularity
                2.   Sports and ideology
        C.   Additional consequences of high schools sports
                1.   Getting noticed and rewarded
                2.   Attracting adult advocates
                3.   Providing occasions for learning

III.   Intercollegiate sports and the experiences of college students
        (BOX: "Intercollegiate sports are not all the same")
        A.   Student-athletes in "big-time" programs
        (BOX: "Making choices: The experiences of athletes in 'big-time' programs")
        B.   Grades and graduation rates: how do athletes compare with other college
                students?
        C.   Recent changes in big-time intercollegiate sports

IV.   Do schools benefit from varsity sports programs?
        A.   School spirit
        B.   School budgets
                1.   High schools
                2.   Colleges and universities
        C.   School-community relations

V.   Varsity high school sports: problems and recommendations
        A.   Overemphasis on "sports development" and "big-time" program models
                1.   Recommendations
        B.   Limited participation access
                1.   Recommendations
        C.   Emphasis on conformity and obedience rather than responsibility and
                autonomy
                1.   Recommendations

MULTIPLE CHOICE QUESTIONS

1.   Research shows that when high school athletes as a group are compared to other high school students, they tend to have
    a.   lower grades but higher educational aspirations
    b.   higher grades and higher educational aspirations*
    c.   lower grades and lower educational aspirations
    d.   higher grades and lower educational aspirations

2.   According to the author, the most logical explanation for academic differences between athletes and nonathletes in high school is that
    a.   interscholastic sports attract students with certain characteristics*
    b.   participation in varsity sports builds academic skills
    c.   it takes intelligence to play sports
    d.   sports help students focus on their studies

3.   Research done by Elmer Spreitzer tracked students over a number of years. Spreitzer found that the students who try out for varsity sports, get selected on teams, and then stay on teams are different from other students. They are different in that they
    a.   come from lower socio-economic backgrounds
    b.   have better employment records
    c.   are more disliked by teachers outside of physical education
    d.   have above average self-esteem*

4.   In general, the research on high school sport participation suggests that
    a.   high school sports have nothing to do with the rest of student life at the school
    b.   care should be taken when generalizing about the educational value of school sports*
    c.   playing sports is clearly more educational than participating in other extracurricular activities
    d.   athletes are treated negatively by most teachers in high school

5. Varsity sports are socially significant activities in many high schools, especially in North America. This means that participation on varsity sport teams can contribute to a student's popularity. Research shows that sport participation
   a. destroys students' popularity if they also get very good grades
   b. usually must be combined with other things for it to increase a girl's popularity*
   c. is more important for the popularity of girls than for the popularity of boys
   d. does not lead to popularity when a student also gets good grades

6. In the discussion of student culture in high schools, the author notes that
   a. most high school students think varsity athletics are childish activities
   b. sport involvement is not related to popularity among girls
   c. the "physical capital" gained by high school athletes has a higher "cash-in" value for young women than for young men
   d. academic success is generally important to the majority of high school students whether they play sports or not*

7. According to the text, when it comes to life outside of the classroom, adolescents are concerned with four things. Which of the following is *not* one of those things?
   a. achieving records in at least two sport activities*
   b. achieving social acceptance among peers
   c. developing personal autonomy and growing up into adults
   d. developing a secure sexual identity

8. When journalist H.G. Bissinger studied the football team in a well-known Texas high school, he found that high school football was organized in ways that
   a. challenged traditional ideas about gender and gender roles
   b. reaffirmed traditional racial ideology among whites and produced racial resentment among African Americans*
   c. led football players to be selfish and unconcerned about the team's fate
   d. ultimately led to a re-establishment of racial segregation in the schools

9. Anthropologist Doug Foley studied a small Texas town and found that high school sports gave students a vocabulary that identified important values and experiences. This vocabulary generally promoted values emphasizing
   a. cooperation
   b. similarities between men and women
   c. individualism*
   d. the meaninglessness of social class

10. The author argues that varsity sports can be valuable in the educational process when they are organized to emphasize certain things. Which of the following is *not* one of the factors identified by the author in his discussion of what makes sports educational? Sports are educational when
   a. they help young people connect with adults who can serve as their advocates
   b. they are purposely turned into learning experiences by teachers
   c. they enable young people to develop and display their competence in the community
   d. they receive special advantages in the classroom and in the community as a whole*

11. In the author's comparison of big-time and lower-profile intercollegiate sport programs it is concluded that
   a. both types of programs are basically the same when it comes to rewards associated with participation
   b. most athletes in lower-profile programs do not have athletic scholarships*
   c. nearly all athletes in big-time programs have professional sport careers after they graduate
   d. most U.S. colleges and universities have big-time sports programs

12. Male athletes on intercollegiate teams are most likely to put their athletic and social lives ahead of academics when they
   a. are majoring in engineering or business
   b. play on big-time, entertainment-oriented teams*
   c. come from wealthy families
   d. are not on athletic scholarships

13. Among male athletes in big-time college sport programs, there is a tendency for athletic identities to be given a higher priority than academic identities because of
   a. feedback received from faculty members on the campuses
   b. their low I.Q. levels
   c. the social support they receive for athletic participation*
   d. personality factors common to most athletes

14. In the special boxed section on "Making Choices," the study done by the Adlers indicated that the male athletes in a big-time intercollegiate basketball program
   a. were often drawn away from academic life after one or two semesters*
   b. came to college with no intention of being serious about academic work
   c. gradually learned to choose their courses in terms of what they thought would offer them academic challenges
   d. interacted so much with nonathletes that they were distracted from their athletic goals

15. In the special boxed section on "Making Choices," the study done by B. Meyer suggested that female volleyball and basketball players in a big-time intercollegiate program
    a. gradually developed anti-intellectual norms among themselves
    b. were more concerned with pro sport careers than getting their degrees
    c. often quit sports to focus on academic achievement and their social lives
    d. generally received support for academic achievement from their teammates*

16. According to the author, the different findings for male and female intercollegiate athletes as reported in the special section on "Making Choices" are probably due to the fact that
    a. women are more concerned about their lives than men are
    b. female athletes get different types of encouragement than men do*
    c. male athletes are not taken seriously by others
    d. women athletes take easier courses than male athletes take

17. Research on the experiences of male intercollegiate athletes indicates that "clustering" occurs when athletes in certain sports
    a. sit together in their classes
    b. are over-represented in specific courses and majors*
    c. get the same grades even when take different courses
    d. join the same fraternities

18. After reading the section on the graduation rates of college athletes, it would be reasonable to conclude that the rates would be lowest for
    a. black male athletes in revenue producing sports*
    b. white male athletes in minor sports
    c. all athletes in minor sports
    d. black women athletes in swimming and tennis

19. Data on graduation rates indicates that
    a. college athletes with scholarships graduate at a lower rate than other students
    b. women playing on entertainment-oriented university teams have experienced a recent decline in their graduation rates*
    c. graduation rates for black male athletes are lower than they are for other black men in the same universities
    d. universities with the highest-ranked sport teams have the best graduation rates among athletes

20. According to the author, statistics on graduation rates are best seen as indicators of
    a. which schools should be put on probation by the NCAA
    b. what needs to be done to correct problems in intercollegiate sports
    c. possible problems and the need for action*
    d. the integrity of the faculty at colleges and universities

21. According to the author, the new trend toward corporate sponsorships in intercollegiate sports will
    a. encourage athletes to take their academic work more seriously
    b. put more emphasis on non-educational issues in sport programs*
    c. lead to the provision of high tech academic support programs for athletes
    d. help athletes get good jobs in the off-season

22. According to the author, the purpose of the many changes that have occurred in connection with intercollegiate sports in the U.S. has been to
    a. eliminate special academic support programs for student-athletes
    b. make coaches more aware of the importance of sports on major college campuses
    c. encourage student-athletes and athletic departments to give high priority to academic standards*
    d. develop special ACT and SAT tests for student-athletes

23. According to the author, in order for the student spirit created by interscholastic sports to take on any academic significance in high school, it must be
    a. heavily promoted by school authorities
    b. a part of an overall school program that makes students feel like valued participants*
    c. associated with winning teams and occasional state championships
    d. expressed in ways that attract media attention

24. According to the author, what percentage of high school budgets are used to maintain varsity sport programs?
    a. 10-15%
    b. 25-30%
    c. 5-8%
    d. 1-3%*

25. Financial information on big-time intercollegiate sport programs shows that they
    a. usually generate enough profits to support academic programs
    b. lead wealthy alumni to give money to academic programs at the universities with the best varsity sport records
    c. usually lose money, even when they include football*
    d. only lose money when they are located in the same town as professional football and basketball teams

26. The studies that have been done on the relationship between intercollegiate sports and financial support from alumni suggest that big-time intercollegiate sport programs
    a. are essential for maintaining high contribution rates
    b. could be dropped without affecting alumni attachments to the school
    c. generate money for academic as well as athletic programs
    d. do not generate money to support education and research*

27. The author notes that when intercollegiate sports are used in connection with fund-raising by colleges and universities, care must be taken to
   a. avoid creating an image that the university is a "sports factory"*
   b. prevent donors from meeting athletes
   c. introduce donors to all coaches, even for the low-profile sports
   d. create an image emphasizing gender equity in the sports program as a whole

28. According to the author, interscholastic sport programs have done two things in the realm of school-community relations. They have
   a. attracted attention and provided entertainment*
   b. generated revenue and created advertising possibilities
   c. encouraged real estate speculation and commercial investment in communities
   d. provided occupational opportunities for local students

29. Which of the following was *not* included by the author as one of the major problems facing high school sport programs?
   a. the tendency to overemphasize "big-time" program models
   b. providing too few participation opportunities for students
   c. using academic funds to hire athletic trainers*
   d. putting too much emphasis on conformity and obedience

30. One of the author's major recommendations for high school sport programs is
   a. eliminating all contact sports for boys and girls
   b. increasing participation opportunities and decision-making by students*
   c. using gate receipts and fund-raising procedures for financing programs
   d. emphasizing state tournaments rather than city tournaments

31. Data on the participation rates of boys and girls in interscholastic sports show that the number of
   a. girls participating has now surpassed the number of boys participating
   b. girls participating has increased but remains much lower than the number of boys participating*
   c. participants among both boys and girls has steadily declined since the early 1970s
   d. girls participating has increased every year since the early 1970s while the number of boys participating has not changed

32. A review of the history of intercollegiate sport programs shows that commercialism and professionalization
   a. have only become problems in recent years
   b. were never problems prior to World War II
   c. have been regular problems for the past century*
   d. have never been studied until the 1970s

33. According to the author's analysis of problems connected with intercollegiate programs,
    a. gender inequity remains a major problem*
    b. problems related to athletes' rights have been eliminated over the past few years
    c. poor coaching is the major problem in most colleges and universities
    d. too many African American athletes are being recruited by intercollegiate programs

34. According to the recommendations for intercollegiate sport made by the author, student-athletes should
    a. have stricter limits put on their financial aid awards
    b. lose their scholarships if coaches feel they are not contributing to the success of their teams
    c. receive need-based financial assistance over and above their athletic scholarships*
    d. be expected to provide their own medical and dental insurance before they are allowed to play sports

35. According to data on gender equity in Division I colleges and universities, women's sports receive
    a. a share of money equal to the proportion of women in the student body as a whole
    b. nearly half of all operating expenses in athletic departments
    c. less money in 1996 than they received back in 1970
    d. less than 30% of all money spent on recruiting expenses*

36. After reviewing data on race and intercollegiate sports in Division I colleges and universities, the author concludes that
    a. black athletes receive too many scholarships in football and basketball and not enough in track and field
    b. colleges and universities don't take blacks seriously as athletes even though they give many scholarships to blacks
    c. colleges and universities have distorted priorities when it comes to race relations and education*
    d. the proportion of college administrators and faculty who are black is actually higher than the proportion of football scholarships awarded to black student-athletes

37. According to data presented in the chapter, over 90% of black male athletes participate in
    a. volleyball, basketball, and football
    b. football, basketball, and track and field*
    c. track and field, basketball, and baseball
    d. baseball, basketball, and football

38. One of the main problems faced by African American student-athletes on college campuses is a feeling of isolation. According to the material presented in the chapter, which of the following factors does *not* contribute to feelings of isolation?
    a. a lack of academic networking through which black student-athletes are connected with other students
    b. too many campus activities related to the interests of African Americans*
    c. racial and athletic stereotypes used by some people on campus
    d. cultural differences between black student-athletes and other students

---

ESSAY QUESTIONS

1. You are a reporter for the local newspaper in your midwestern U.S. town. Due to a serious budget crisis, the local school board is contemplating dropping all varsity sport programs. The board has scheduled a meeting to discuss this issue with community people, some of whom are proponents of the programs, and some of whom feel that sports should be dropped to save other programs. To prepare for the meeting, you are reviewing the arguments you expect to hear on both sides of the issue. What are those arguments, and who do you expect to be the most vocal proponents of each?

2. You are a member of an urban school board. The board has just been presented with data showing that varsity athletes in the 15 high schools in your district receive higher grades than nonathletes. The data are being used by a parent group who want more funds for interscholastic sports in the district. What are the questions you would ask about the data, and why would you ask them?

3. The principal in your school has announced that she is thinking of dropping all interscholastic sports because they distort the basis for popularity in the high school by focusing attention on something other than academic achievement. As a coach you disagree with the principal. Put together an argument that would lead her to change her mind on this issue.

4. Varsity sports provide experiences through which high school student learn things about culture and cultural ideology in the U.S. According to research done on high school sports, what are the "cultural lessons" emphasized in connection with high school football?

5. The academic experiences of student-athletes in colleges with big-time sport programs are different than the experiences of student-athletes in colleges with lower-profile programs. If you were talking to a group of high school seniors interested in playing college sports, how would you explain these differences?

6. You are appointed academic advisor for both the men's and women's basketball teams at a major university with a big-time sport program. What patterns of academic involvement will you expect from the student-athletes on these teams, and how will these patterns affect your program as an advisor?

7. For the past 15 years, you have been the academic advisor for the women's sport teams at your university. The women's basketball and volleyball teams have been to the NCAA tournament every year for the past five years; each team has won the national title once during that five-year period. You notice that your athletes are having more academic problems than ever before. In fact, their academic patterns have begun to resemble the patterns of the men on the basketball and football teams. How do you explain this change? Is it a short-term change, or a more permanent one?

8. While you are at home during the semester break, you are watching a football bowl game with your mother. She says that it is terrible that student-athletes have such poor graduation records. You tell her that graduation rates among student-athletes are not as bad as she thinks. She asks you to explain. What do you tell her?

9. Recent changes in big-time intercollegiate sports have been encouraging to people interested in academic standards. Describe some of those changes and highlight what still needs to be done when it comes to increasing the educational relevance of big-time intercollegiate sport programs.

10. For many years, interscholastic sports have been used to generate school spirit in high schools and colleges in the United States. If those programs were dropped, could spirit still be generated? Give some examples of how spirit could be generated through alternatives to interscholastic sports.

11. You are on the president's advisory board for a mid-sized state university with about 12,000 students. The president says that the financial future of the school depends on developing a higher profile among the people of the state, including everyone from high school students to state legislators and business leaders. He says that the way to make and raise more money is to invest in a high-profile varsity sports program. He asks you to discuss the pros and cons of this strategy. What do you say?

12. Your university president has recommended the expansion of a couple of high profile varsity sports so they can be used for public relations and fundraising. You are asked by the student newspaper to respond to the recommendation. What would your response be? (Use material in the chapter.)

13. Using your own university as an example, discuss how its varsity sport programs affect school-community relations. How is the impact of a university program different than the impact of a high school program when it comes to school-community relations?

162

14. After reading about the problems in high school sport programs and the recommendations for change suggested by the author, describe which problems existed in the high school you attended during your senior year. Then suggest two recommendations that would make your old high school program better and explain how the recommendations would improve things.

15. After reading about the problems in intercollegiate sport programs and the recommendations for change suggested by the author, describe which problems exist in your college or university right now. Then list four recommendations that would improve your intercollegiate program and explain how the recommendations would improve things.

16. Faculty at your former high school have suggested replacing the varsity sports programs with a number of student-run club sports, including some sports that are co-educational, such as doubles tennis, forms of volleyball, track and field, in-line skating, and other sports that men and women would compete in together under conditions that would insure equal contributions by men and women to team success. The faculty say that this will not only develop leadership skills among students, but it will provide a setting for the development of social skills. Would you support such an innovation, or oppose it? Explain your position.

17. Gender inequity is still one of the major problems affecting intercollegiate sport programs in the U.S. Using the men's and the women's programs at your own school as examples, show whether inequities exist at your school. Regardless of your conclusion, give examples to back up your position.

18. "Intercollegiate student-athletes need a union to lobby for changes in how they are treated in sport programs." This is a controversial statement. Use material from the chapter and from your own experience to either support this statement or to argue against it.

19. With the decline of affirmative action programs, the number of African American students in the general student body at your university is down. But the number of African American athletes in the revenue producing sports is up. This has led some people to say that your university cares little about the educational needs of African Americans unless they have athletic abilities that can be exploited. What could be done at your university to avoid this criticism?

20. The intercollegiate sport programs at your school are in bad financial shape. Because of large losses, the students have been asked to increase their student fees by $100 per semester to maintain the programs. If the fee increase does not pass, all the intercollegiate sport programs are scheduled to be dropped and replaced by low-cost, student-run club sports. How would you vote? Use material from the chapter to give reasons for your decision.

CHAPTER 15
SPORTS AND RELIGION:
is it a promising combination?

CHAPTER OUTLINE

MULTIPLE CHOICE QUESTIONS

1. Sociologists study religion because religious systems of meaning
    a. contain principles of ultimate truth that determine social relations
    b. affect the way people think about the world and about their relationships with other people*
    c. force people to ignore ultimate issues and questions
    d. identify the way a culture must be organized if it is be meaningful and successful

2. According to the author, religious systems of meaning are socially significant because they have an impact on
    a. who is accorded moral power and authority in a culture*
    b. the location of sport facilities within communities
    c. which sports are played by certain groups of people
    d. the levels of violence that are tolerated in different cultures

3. Some people argue that sports and religion overlap in certain ways. Theologian Michael Novak has made the case that sports are forms of godliness because
    a. they are male dominated in most cultures
    b. they emerge out of the same quest for perfection that is the basis for conceptions of god in a culture*
    c. involve the participation of people who have committed themselves to a set of ideals about goodness
    d. can be traced back to specific religious rituals in Western civilization

4. Those who see sports as forms of religion identify similarities between sports and Judeo-Christian religious systems of meaning. Which of the following is *not* one of the similarities between religion and sports that these people tend to identify?
    a. both are based on beliefs about human weakness*
    b. both have heroes and legends about the accomplishments of those heroes
    c. both have procedures and dramas linked to personal betterment
    d. both emphasize asceticism and self-discipline

5. According to the author, most people who believe that religion and sport have essential, but different, characteristics, say that the rituals and beliefs of religion are always
    a. related to what it takes to be successful in a society
    b. based on general superstitions in a culture
    c. preserved in written forms
    d. connected to the sacred and supernatural*

6. Many people believe there are "essential" differences between sport and religion. According to the author, many of these "essentialists" would see sport as
    a. expressive while religion is instrumental
    b. based on a spirit of self-promotion while religion is based on a spirit of service and love*
    c. grounded in commonly held beliefs while religion is grounded in diversified beliefs
    d. competitive and communal while religion is noncompetitive and individualistic

7. When social constructionists study sports and religions, they usually assume that the systems of meanings associated with each of these spheres of life
    a. emphasize issues of social integration
    b. tend to celebrate the ideologies of people who challenge dominant ideas in society
    c. change over time and vary from one group to another*
    d. are based people's ideas about the sacred and supernatural

8. In the author's discussion of sports and religions around the world, he notes that
    a. Buddhist athletes have set more international records than Christian athletes
    b. Hinduism emphasizes the use of physical discipline to achieve greatness in sports
    c. there are relatively few women athletes from countries where Muslim and Hindu beliefs are prevalent*
    d. all religions are connected with sports in similar ways around the world

9. In the author's analysis of "the Protestant Ethic and the Spirit of Sports," he argues that sports in industrialized societies tend to bring together a cultural emphasis on rationality and hard work with a corresponding emphasis on
    a. celebrating the body's productive potential*
    b. the use of the body for pleasure
    c. making money and having fun
    d. the importance of following the scriptures

10. Christians and Christian organizations have used sports to promote spiritual growth and certain types of religious beliefs. According to the author, they have also used sports to
    a. identify people who lack spiritual worth
    b. encourage people to challenge traditional definitions of masculinity and femininity
    c. highlight the existence of social problems and the need for social action
    d. recruit new members to their organizations and belief systems*

11. In recent years, there has been a growth in religious-sport organizations. In general, these organizations tend to be
   a. concerned with social issues and social change
   b. outreach groups for major Christian denominations such as Lutherans and Methodists
   c. grounded in non-Christian belief systems
   d. based on conservative, fundamentalist Christian orientations*

12. Some athletes have used religion to deal with the uncertainty they face during sport participation. When this is done, the author notes that religion
   a. becomes a form of self-glorification
   b. serves purposes similar to those served by magic and superstition*
   c. becomes as important as referees in influencing the outcomes of events
   d. makes athletes so relaxed that they perform poorly

13. According to anthropologist Mari Womack (in a boxed section), rituals are widely used in sports because
   a. athletes are biologically predisposed to be superstitious
   b. rituals focus individual motivations and needs on the achievement of group goals*
   c. rituals create uncertainty that leads to motivation
   d. athletes enjoy repetition, and rituals are always repetitive

14. The author notes that in sports characterized by risky lifestyles, athletes have sometimes used religion to
   a. gain endorsement contracts for wholesome products
   b. enable them to take risks without consequences
   c. strengthen their relationships with athletes who have problems
   d. generally stay out of trouble*

15. The author argues that because sport participation is based on self-promotion, athletes may sometimes combine sport participation with religious beliefs to
   a. give sport participation special meaning*
   b. gain support from fellow believers
   c. decrease the importance of following the direction of coaches
   d. turn sports into forms of social service

16. The author points out that religion can become a means of social control in sports when
   a. athletes use religious beliefs to raise moral issues about sports
   b. parents encourage their children to be Christian athletes
   c. the quality of sport performance is connected with the moral worth of athletes*
   d. athletes say private prayers to avoid injuries

17. According to the Institute for Athletic Perfection, a "Total Release Performance" (TRP) involves
    a. complete obedience to one's coach*
    b. an emphasis on service
    c. a focus on democracy in coach-athlete relationships
    d. raising questions about coach's rules

18. The author argues that combining traditional Christian religious beliefs with the dominant forms of sports in many societies is sometimes difficult because Christianity emphasizes
    a. aggression while sports emphasize following rules
    b. humility and service to others while sports emphasize focusing on the self and achieving personal success*
    c. sacrificing one's body for the goal of success while sports emphasize training the body
    d. that bodies are weak while sports emphasize that bodies are strong

19. Using material from Shirl Hoffman's book, *Sport and Religion*, the author notes that certain aspects of power and performance sports raise questions about whether participation in these sports should be used as acts of worship. Which of the following is *not* one of the aspects of sports that raise these questions?
    a. self-promotion and the aggressive pursuit of personal success
    b. converting the human body in a performance machine
    c. the use of violence and intimidation
    d. the importance of keeping score in games played with other people*

20. According to the "model of conflict, doubt, and resolution" diagrammed in the chapter, Christian athletes who experience doubts about the worth of sport participation as a symbolic religious offering can ease those doubts through three main resolution strategies. Which of the following is *not* one of those strategies?
    a. developing friendships with non-Christian athletes*
    b. ignoring the moral questions related to behavior on the playing field
    c. focusing on the ascetic dimensions of athletic training and performance
    d. focusing on good works and service to others off the field

21. Research suggests that many Christian athletes avoid conflicts related to their religious beliefs and sport participation by
    a. questioning game rules in their sports and the rules of coaches
    b. playing sports differently than they are played by athletes who do not profess Christian beliefs
    c. becoming involved in political organizations that want to change sports
    d. playing with "the right attitude" and emphasizing obedience to game rules*

22. According to the policy positions of most of the major religious-sport organizations, the social and ethical problems in sports will continue to exist until
    a.   competition is eliminated from sport activities
    b.   the media provide accurate information about sports
    c.   all people in sports have a personal faith in Christ*
    d.   rules are changed in the sport organizations themselves

23. In discussing the effects of combining sports and religion (especially Christianity), the author concludes that the combination has usually led to
    a.   a reaffirmation of the existing characteristics of dominant sports*
    b.   revolutionary changes in athletes' behaviors
    c.   a decline in aggressive behavior and competitive spirit among athletes and coaches
    d.   a decrease in the injury rates among athletes

ESSAY QUESTIONS

1. One of your humanities teachers has just said that sport is the newest and fastest-growing religion in North America. Would you agree or disagree with this statement? Is sport a form of religion?

2. It is the year 2525. All life forms have died out on planet Earth. A group of archaeologists and anthropologists from another planet come to explore Earth. In one of their digs, they unearth the Superdome in what was once New Orleans. After going through all the artifacts they find, they conclude that the people in this area must have been very religious. How might they come to such a conclusion? How could they mistakenly conclude that a sport stadium and sport activities were indicators of religion?

3. The "essentialists" and the "social constructionists" view the connection between sports and religions in different ways. Which approach do you think provides a more useful understanding of sports and religions? Which approach would you use if you were studying sports and religions around the world?

4. The author makes the case that sports have been incorporated into Christian organizations and beliefs because sports and Christianity emphasize a rationally controlled lifestyle characterized by discipline, hard work, sacrifice, and the endurance of pain. Why is such an emphasis important in certain cultures, and how does sport participation fit with a rationally controlled lifestyle?

5. Christians and Christian organizations have used sports to promote spiritual growth, to recruit new members, and to promote fundamentalist beliefs. Using your own community or experience as a point of focus, explain whether sports have been used in any of these ways by Christians or Christian organizations with which you are familiar.

6. The pastor of your church/congregation has just asked everyone for a donation to help purchase advertising time on the Super Bowl next January. Evangelical churches all around the U.S. are participating in this fundraising effort. The goal is to associate Christian beliefs with the most popular cultural event in the U.S. so that new members, especially men, can be recruited into certain religious organizations. Explain some of the sociological issues underlying this fundraising campaign. Would you donate your money to such a cause?

7. The uncertainty that exists in sports has often led people involved in sports to use religion, magic, and superstition in connection with their sport lives. Using your own experience, provide examples showing that any or all of these might be related to controlling uncertainty.

8. Religious beliefs and rituals are potentially powerful in the lives of individuals. This is one of the reasons why they are used in connection with sport participation. According to the author, what are the major reasons why athletes in the U.S. and a few other countries have combined certain forms of Christian beliefs and rituals with their sport participation? Do you agree or disagree with the author's list of reasons?

9. The author notes that there are some potential problems associated with coaches combining religion with sport participation on their teams. When is this combination most likely to be the source of problems?

10. The author concludes that the combination of Christian religious beliefs and sports has not lead to any significant changes in the way sports are organized and played. Do you agree or disagree with this conclusion? Give your reasons and provide examples from your own experience.

11. Imagine that you are a Christian boxer. How can you combine your religious beliefs and your participation in your sport? What kinds of problems would you have in making this combination? What are the origins of those problems?

12. An upcoming heavyweight boxing title fight involves a Christian boxer who claims to be fighting for Jesus Christ and his God, and an Moslem boxer who claims to be fighting for Mohammed and Allah. Both say they are merely instruments of their Supreme Being as they fight in the ring; they also say that what they do to prepare for the fight and what they do in the ring is basically a form of religious witness. What are the sociological issues raised by these claims? Do you see any problems with such a combination of religion and sport? Explain.

13. Your best friend is a football player who says that he lives his religion during the football season by "hitting my opponents with all the love of Jesus I have in me." You are familiar with basic Christian theology, and his combination of football and religion does not seem to be consistent with what you know about the teachings of Christ. You are curious about how he reconciles the conflicts you see in his approach. What questions do you ask him, and how do you expect he might respond?

14. When Christian athletes see conflicts between their religious beliefs and the way dominant forms of sports are played, how do they deal with or resolve those conflicts? What forms of coping or resolution do you think are most common among the athletes you've met in your experience?

15. "Combining Christian religious beliefs with sport participation is the only way we can make sports into more humane activities." Respond to this statement in light of the material in the chapter and your own experiences.

CHAPTER 16
SPORTS IN THE FUTURE:
what can we expect?

CHAPTER OUTLINE

I.   Major sport forms in the future
    A.   Power and performance sports
    B.   Pleasure and participation sports

II.   Future trends in sports
    A.   The growth of power and performance sports
    B.   The growth of pleasure and participation sports
    C.   Growing concerns about health and fitness
    D.   Participation preferences among older people
    E.   Women bringing new values and experiences to sports
    F.   Groups seeking alternative sports
    (BOX: "What will happen if more people play sports?")

III.   Specific forecasts
    A.   Professional sports
    B.   Intercollegiate sports
    C.   High school sports
    D.   Youth sports
    E.   Spectators and spectator sports
    F.   Organization and rationalization
    G.   Commercialism and consumerism
    H.   Technology and media

IV.   Conclusion: The challenge of making the future
    A.   Three approaches to change
    B.   Four vantage points for making change
    (BOX: "Athletes as change agents: does it ever happen?")

MULTIPLE CHOICE QUESTIONS

1. In the introduction to the chapter, the author points out that the future of sports will
   a. emerge in an uncontrollable manner
   b. involve such dramatic changes that most of us will be surprised and shocked
   c. have little to do with general social conditions
   d. be shaped by people making choices about what they want sports to be*

2. When considering the future, the author suggests that we remember two things. One is that the future is not determined by fate, and the other is that
   a. some sports will always exist in a pure form
   b. capitalism and team sports go hand-in-hand
   c. competition is a part of human nature
   d. sports are contested activities*

3. The author notes that at any particular point in time in a culture, dominant sport forms
   a. tend to reflect the interests of those who have power in that culture*
   b. involve more of an emphasis on speed than strength
   c. are more closely tied to the lives of working-class people than to upper-class people
   d. appeal more to the interests of spectators than to the athletes themselves

4. The author predicts that power and performance sports will continue to be visible and publicized forms of sport in the near future. Power and performance sports tend to emphasize the idea that human beings reach their potential when they
   a. achieve machine-like efficiency*
   b. develop close, personal relationships with their coaches and fellow competitors
   c. achieve excellence in terms of personal enjoyment
   d. use physical skills and sports as a source of personal empowerment

5. The sponsorship of power and performance sports is generally motivated by the idea that it is important to be associated with
   a. masses of people participating in sports
   b. athletes and teams who are currently winners*
   c. athletes who do community service work
   d. groups of spectators known for their enthusiastic support of sports

6. According to the author's description, pleasure and participation sports generally emphasize
   a. exclusive forms of participation
   b. the achievement of competitive success
   c. an ethic of good health*
   d. the body as a machine that must be kept well tuned

7. When people play pleasure and participation sports, they are likely to
   a. find it easy to get corporate sponsorships
   b. focus on their connections with other participants*
   c. avoid all forms of physical exertion
   d. prefer indoor sports over outdoor sports

8. The classic embodiment of power and performance sports is
   a. Ultimate Frisbee
   b. co-rec softball
   c. international cricket
   d. American football*

9. According to the author, the popularity of power and performance sports is tied to gender relations because these sports tend to
   a. emphasize co-recreational participation
   b. celebrate the physical superiority of men over women*
   c. give women a chance to surpass the performances of men
   d. attract more female spectators than male spectators

10. The author notes that if power and performance sports continue to be popular, we can expect that
    a. sports will reproduce ideas emphasizing physical differences between men and women*
    b. women's sports will eventually become as popular as men's sports
    c. there will be decreased concerns with gender issues
    d. women will begin to outperform men in certain sports based on strength and speed

11. Power and performance sports are sometimes combined with technology. The author describes these combinations as "technosports." According to the author, technosports are characterized by
    a. an emphasis on freedom and spontaneity among athletes
    b. strong spectator identification with athletes
    c. pushing human limits in the pursuit of performance records*
    d. a strong element of play that replaces the desire to dominate opponents

12. The author suggests that the use of technology in sports may be limited in the future by
    a. the refusal of sport promoters and sponsors to fund the development of sport technology
    b. governmental restrictions on the use of technology in society as a whole
    c. the possibility that spectators will not identify with athletes produced by technology*
    d. the inability of athletes to gain access to new forms of technology

13. According to the author, pleasure and participation sports are likely to become increasingly popular in the future because
    a. the average age of the population is getting younger and younger
    b. more women are looking to men as models for how to do sports
    c. fewer people are looking for alternatives to dominant sport forms
    d. there are growing concerns about how physical activities can improve health and fitness*

14. According to the author, the Gay Games are an example of
    a. an extreme form of power and performance sports
    b. a group seeking an alternative to dominant sport forms*
    c. people who want to avoid competition in their sports
    d. sports being used to support dominant ideas about sexuality

15. There are a number of predictions made in the chapter. Which of the following is *not* one of the author's predictions?
    a. the consumption of brand-name clothing and equipment will continue to be important
    b. high schools will eliminate play-offs and state championship tournaments in all varsity sports*
    c. the power and autonomy of professional athletes will increase
    d. publicly funded youth sports programs will be cut back or eliminated in many communities

16. The author predicts that
    a. sport spectators will stop betting on the outcomes of games
    b. professional sport teams in most countries will stop recruiting athletes from other countries
    c. there will be an increase in the use of "technical specialists" to improve sport performance*
    d. sport participation will become less organized and more spontaneous

17. In the box titled, "What will happen if more people play sports?" the author predicts that if sport participation rates continue to increase in the future, we can expect certain things to happen. According to the model presented, an increase in mass sport participation will be associated with
    a. increased cooperation between participants from all backgrounds
    b. increased regulation of sport facilities by public and private agencies*
    c. a growth in sports based on the Pleasure and Participation Model
    d. a growth in the number of facilities people can use without paying fees

18. According to the author's predictions (in the boxed section), as mass participation in sports increases, there will be a greater tendency for sports to
    a. remain highly organized and competitive*
    b. become less commercialized and less organized
    c. change in an unpredictable ways
    d. become less and less elitist in the way they are organized

175

19. In the discussion of different approaches to social change, the author notes that reformists are primarily concerned with
   a. doing away with sports altogether
   b. preventing the use of technology in sports
   c. making sports more fair and equitable*
   d. expanding sports as they are currently organized

20. In the discussion of different approaches to social change, it was pointed out that the radical approach is primarily concerned with
   a. creating new models for organizing and playing sports*
   b. doing away with sports altogether
   c. raising funds to support more sports for more people
   d. promoting the growth of power and performance sports

21. A conservative approach to social change in sports generally emphasizes
   a. the elimination of all sports that are not profit-making
   b. using sports to teach cooperation and sensitivity
   c. changing sports to how they were before 1900
   d. the growth and efficiency of existing sport programs*

22. Radical approaches to change in sports are rarely used because radicals
   a. tend to avoid physical activities in their own lives
   b. are more concerned with basic living conditions issues rather than sports*
   c. realize that sports are not related to ideological issues in society
   d. avoid confrontation and competition in their lives

23. There are four different vantage points for making changes in sports. Which of the following does *not* describe one of those vantage points?
   a. creating alternative sports in the community
   b. joining groups opposed to dominant sports in society
   c. focusing on issues related to social relations and then raising questions about how sports are organized
   d. trying to be the best you can be within a sport*

24. The author argues that when highly visible and popular athletes become involved in efforts to make change, they usually take which type of approach?
   a. conservative*
   b. reformist
   c. radical
   d. a combination of reformist and radical

25. According to the author's discussion of athletes as change agents, which of the following change efforts would a pro basketball player be most likely to join?
   a. a civil rights group that supports affirmative action
   b. a political group lobbying for curriculum changes in a school district
   c. a program to improve reading skills among low-income children*
   d. a group advocating a program to eliminate poverty in a community

26. According to the author, making changes in sports is difficult because significant social transformations depend on a combination of three things: (1) a vision of what sports and social life could and should be, (2) a willingness to work hard, and (3)

    a.   a personal history of success as an athlete
    b.   a good reputation among people in sports
    c.   a job in a large, influential sport organization
    d.   an ability to rally the resources needed to produce results*

ESSAY QUESTIONS

1. One of your friends does not understand the distinctions between power and performance sports and pleasure and participation sports. Use your own experience to explain the differences to your friends, and then indicate which sports you would prefer to participate in and why.

2. According to the author's predictions, if athletes take more and more specialized substances, both natural and manufactured, and use more sophisticated equipment to develop skills, watching sports may become less interesting for spectators. How does the author come to this conclusion? Do you agree with the reasoning underlying this conclusion?

3. The use of technology in sports will not simply be the result of what is technologically possible. In other words, some people will raise questions about the use of certain forms of technology in sports. What are some of the questions that people have raised about the use of technology in sports over the past 10 years? What are forms of technology that you think will be questioned over the next 10 years?

4. There is a debate scheduled for your next sociology of sport class. The thesis being proposed and supported by one debate team is that corporations have stronger vested interests in sponsoring power and performance sports than they do in sponsoring pleasure and participation sports. The other team will argue the opposite thesis: that corporations have a stronger vested interest in sponsoring pleasure and participation sports. Which side do you think will win? Give reasons for your choice.

5. The author suggests that in the future there will be increased participation in pleasure and participation sports. Four factors are given as reasons for this increased growth. Focusing on your own community, discuss whether these reasons will have an impact on how sports are defined, organized, and played in the future; indicate which factor will have the most impact on the growth of pleasure and participation sports in your community.

6. More and more people in your community are participating in sports. Use the author's predictive model (in the special boxed section) and indicate what could happen if sport participation rates increased greatly in the community where you live.

7. According to the predictions made in the first boxed section in the chapter, increased sport participation is likely to lead to various forms of elitism combined with an emphasis on power and performance sports. What forms of intervention could be used at the community level to discourage elitism and encourage participation in pleasure and participation sports?

8. In the material in the boxed section in the chapter, the author indicates that as more people participate in sports, there will be an increasing amount of conflict between groups of participants. Discuss at least two examples from your own experience where this has happened. When it happened, what were the consequences? Did the consequences fit what the author predicted they would be?

9. You are working as an administrator in a local Park and Recreation Department. As more people participate in sports in your city, a serious shortage of spaces and facilities develops. You realize that unless you do something, this scarcity of spaces and facilities will lead to more and more regulations. You also realize that with regulations will come more elitism in sports. You do not want to see this happen. How could you prevent these things from happening?

10. There are a number of general and specific predictions made in Chapter 16. Choose two of the predictions you agree with and two that you disagree with; provide explanations supporting your agreement and disagreement.

11. Using the author's predictions about what will happen to sports during the 21st century, describe what the sports program at your university will look like when your son or daughter is a student there in the year 2030.

12. Using the author's predictions about what will happen to sports during the 21st century, describe what the youth sports in your community will look like when your son or daughter is old enough to play sports in the year 2015.

13. One of your friends says that video technology will totally change spectator experiences over the next 25 years. What forms of video innovations do you think people will find most attractive over the next 25 years? Will young people abandon watching telecasts of live sport events in favor of playing video games that simulate sports? Explain why or why not.

14. Of the three approaches to social change discussed in the concluding section of the chapter, which approach (reformist, radical, or conservative) do you agree with the most, and why? Which approach do you agree with the least, and why?

15. The author (borrowing from the ideas of Hall et al., 1991) suggests that there are four vantage points from which to make changes in sports. Using examples from your university, community, or country, show how changes have been made from each of the four vantage points (from within the system, through participation in oppositional groups, through the creation of alternative sports, and through focusing on culture and social relations). Identify the changes that you think are most significant.

16. People who have focused on making changes in gender relations have had an impact on sports and sport organizations. Using examples from your university, community, or country, show how changes related to gender and gender relations have affected sports and sport organizations.